Small Gardens

INSPIRED PLANTINGS FOR DIMINUTIVE SPACES

Becke Davis

FRIEDMAN/FAIRFAX

PUBLISHERS

A FRIEDMAN/FAIRFAX BOOK

Library of Congress Cataloging-in-Publication Data

Davis, Becke
      Small gardens : inspired plantings for diminuitive spaces / Becke Davis.
p.   cm.
      Includes bibliographical references (p.   ) and index.
      ISBN 1-56799-429-6
      1. Landscape gardening.   2. Gardening.   I. Title.
SB473.D38   1997
712'.6--dc20   96-35753

Editor: Susan Lauzau
Art Director: Jeff Batzli
Photography Editor: Deidra Gorgos
Design and illustration by Amanda Wilson
Garden plan illustrations by Susan Kemritz
Color separations by Ad. Ver. srl.
Printed in China by Leefung Asco Ltd.

10 9 8 7 6 5 4 3 2 1

For bulk purchases and special sales, please contact:
Friedman/Fairfax Publishers
Attention: Sales Department
15 West 26th Street
New York, New York 10010
212/685-6610   FAX 212/685-1307

Visit our website:
http://www.metrobooks.com

To my editor, Susan Lauzau, for her patience and enthusiasm; her careful pruning rejuvenated and renewed.

To Mick Miller, gardener and good friend, gone too soon; Jean Thorpe, balcony gardener extraordinaire; and Pat Schiltz, who understands that "who plants a seed beneath the sod and waits to see, believes in God." To Jeff and Mike Lowecki in their pursuit of excellence in landscaping, and to Jeff Tindall, who achieves excellence on a smaller scale. To Rob Wilkins, for his encouragement and honest criticism. To educators Marge Schaller, who has a "grand and glorious" way with words, and the late, great Richard Calisch, whose demand for excellence pushed his students to their limits.

To Patti and Hank Villars, Thom Villars, Connie Soper, Laura Leonard, Russell Villars, and the rest of the clan. To my husband, Marty, as we enter our quarter century together; to Jessica, who loves music more than she'll ever love flowers; to Jonathan, who loves to dig holes in the dirt; and to Maggie, who may someday inspire me to invent a dog-proof garden.

To all those who love gardens but are afraid they are not expert enough to do it right:

Who loves a garden
Finds within his soul
Life's whole;
He hears the anthem of the soil
While ingrates toil;
And sees beyond his little sphere
The waving fronds of heaven, clear.

—LOUISE SEYMOUR JONES

❦ Contents ❦

Introduction

Science has now confirmed what many have long believed—that some people actually become ill during long winter months without sunshine. What science hasn't proved, but what I firmly believe, is that many of us require a garden in much the same way. Even when my hands are blistered and my mind is bent on demolishing Japanese beetles, there is something about a garden that soothes my soul. As I pore over garden magazines and books, I dream of the garden I could create if only I had acres of land and rich, black soil, not to mention bags of money. Reality is an average suburban lot of hard-packed clay and a gardening budget that is regularly diminished by school clothes and vet bills.

My front yard gets so much sun that when I hang a decorated wreath on the front door, the hot glue melts within hours and the decorations drop off. My backyard is a wooded area at the edge of a farmer's field with poison ivy, messy box elders, a gnarly, fruitless Osage orange, plus black locusts self-seeding all over the place. The backyard is in partial shade and one corner has an underground spring, giving me both the benefit of a tiny, shallow stream and the curse of regular flooding. I live in Cincinnati, balancing between Zones 5 and 6; in the three years I've lived here we've had winter weather down to −24°F (−31°C) with as much as 14 inches (35.5cm) of snow, wet springs, and dry, hot summers that hover in the 90s (32° to 38°C). Just to make gardening more challenging, we get a few February days in the 70s (21° to 26°C). I've talked to gardeners all across North America, and I firmly believe that each place has its unique gardening challenges: too hot or too cold, too wet, too dry, too windy, too much clay, or too much sand. And still the gardens seem to thrive.

Most gardeners are optimists and dreamers, or else how would we ever start with a spot of soil and picture the paradise to come? We gardeners are also artists, scientists, and naturalists, who inevitably become more familiar with bugs than we often would like. Gardeners must be patient, whether we like it or not. And we are pragmatists—no matter how we try to control our gardens, we won't succeed unless we learn to give the plants what they need to survive. Whether a gardener prefers formal rose beds or the wild exuberance of prairie plants, the urge is there: to plan, to plant, to grow. Plant a twig of raspberry and watch it multiply and spread over and around any barrier you put up. See how weeds can sprout from concrete walks and trees can grow out of a rocky ledge. In some gardeners the urge to grow is just as instinctive and just as strong.

Which, in a roundabout way, brings me to the point of this book. A garden does not require acres of rolling countryside—it doesn't even require a piece of ground. City rooftops, apartment balconies, and handkerchief-size townhouse lots can house miniature miracles of plant artistry. Even those blessed with lots of land sometimes feel more comfortable gardening in a manageable space. In the suburbs, it is not uncommon to see miles of neatly groomed lawns accented only by extravagant mailbox gardens and window boxes. Patios, porches, and courtyards also provide perfect areas for plants to bloom, and the plants, in turn, beautify the structure. The maxim "good things come in small packages" is trite but often true; the myriad spaces featured in this book show that a bit of paradise is possible even in a pocket-size garden.

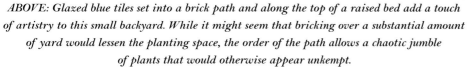

Chapter 1

*ABOVE: Glazed blue tiles set into a brick path and along the top of a raised bed add a touch
of artistry to this small backyard. While it might seem that bricking over a substantial amount
of yard would lessen the planting space, the order of the path allows a chaotic jumble
of plants that would otherwise appear unkempt.*
*ABOVE RIGHT: Purple aubretia spills over stacked stones in this raised bed,
where spring bulbs dwarf a small conifer.*

The Garden in Miniature

Creative Plantings for the Tiny Yard

England, I remember complimenting a gentleman on his lush suburban garden. While accepting my comment as his due, he nodded at my accent and said, "Ah yes, you are from America. You have *yards*." (In England, the word "yard" usually means a paved work area, such as a "brickyard.") I don't think he meant to imbue the word with so much scorn, but it was clear that he envisioned either unadorned squares of lawn, or even worse, concrete. But not all North Americans have "yards," and not all English gardeners have stately homes and acres of land to work with.

Living on the outskirts of London, what impressed me most was not the rarities at Kew, the maze at Hampton Court, or the white garden at Sissinghurst, but rather the ingenious ways Londoners found to beautify their tiny plots with plants. Space is at a premium in London, and it doesn't come cheap—houses split into flats, townhouses clustered around a square, and high-rises with no redeeming architectural value are as common there as in many North American cities; they have just been around longer.

What is a garden? Some people consider a garden nothing but frippery unless it contains a healthy crop of vegetables. Others will accept nothing less than a formal French design or an Italianate garden with marble statuary. Perhaps the humble cottage garden is more to your taste, or maybe you fancy the pleached garden walks of England's stately homes—just look at all the books on English gardens! This must surely be what gardening is all about—or is it?

American and Canadian gardens have long been considered the poor cousins of the older, established English and European gardens. There are exceptions—Winterthur, Filoli, and Butchart Gardens—but for the most part, native woodlands and prairies seem to be the only North American "gardens" that get any respect. When I lived in

ABOVE: A curved path in a small town garden winds past ferns, white marguerites, and variegated mountain flax (Phormium colensoi 'Variegatum'). A garden with mature shrubs like these will provide a screen and sound barrier for neighboring yards.
LEFT: If the heavy-duty maintenance required for a full-scale garden is beyond your time and energy limits, choose instead to plant a border along the front walk or a small island bed in the middle of the front lawn. A jumble of bright flowers mixes happily with foliage plants in this completely manageable space.

With little or no space and a love of gardening, you learn to make the most of what you've got: a balcony; window boxes; window sills; a lilliputian garden nudging a city street; or a narrow, secret garden behind a brownstone. Stone troughs, wooden barrels, wheelbarrows—anything that will hold soil can be planted to overflowing. And the English tradition of making a garden out of nothing is just as visible in North American cities and towns.

This is not to say that gardeners who live in the country or in the suburbs have all the acreage they want; even if they did, in today's world most people don't have the time to maintain an elaborate garden on a day-to-day basis. Small gardens make sense for many reasons—even gardeners lucky enough to have a lot of space may find themselves planting only a few breathtaking beds or a series of small garden "rooms" because they are easier to maintain. By

A lush white garden is filled with 'Noble Maiden' lupines, roses, and other ivory-colored perennials. Note how the creamy variegation of a hosta is enhanced by the pale blooms. All-white gardens are perfect for those who work during the day and enjoy their gardens mainly in the evenings; the white flowers seem to absolutely glow in the moonlight.

LEFT: Vivid flowers in hot colors accent a gold awning and add a Mediterranean flair to this city garden. Without the dense greenery, which contributes an impression of restful coolness, the facade of this house would appear unpleasantly bright. BELOW: The curving brick path and profusion of blooms work together to make this entrance welcoming. An unusual treatment of the classic picket fence features a brilliant display of poppies planted both inside and outside the fence line. When your planting space is small, you must make use of every available bit, so don't overlook curbside strips, driveway borders, and other underused patches of ground.

planting small, beginning gardeners can get to know a few plants at a time, learning their craft without a big outlay or a frightening amount of work.

PLAN YOUR GARDEN TO SUIT YOUR SITE

All right, so any space can become a garden. But can any Larry, Curly, or Moe become a gardener? Certainly—just make sure you are born into a family with generations of gardeners to nurture your skills from childhood. Or be born wealthy so you can hire a wonderful designer and a persnickety but talented gardener to do all the work. Otherwise how can a single person or an average couple with two jobs, 2.5 kids, plus assorted dogs and cats ever find time to master soil science, botany, plant pathology, horticulture, botanical Latin, landscape architecture, arboriculture, color spectrums, weather zones, and microclimates, and all those other things that are integral to gardening? The same way you learned to walk—with baby steps. Start small, learning first about the plants that you love to see if they will work in your garden. Do they require mostly sun or mostly shade? Can they survive the awful weather extremes where you live (everybody has awful weather, with each winter—or summer— worse than the last). Will the plants live if there are watering restrictions? Will you have to bring them inside over the winter? (This can be a real problem with roof gardens and balcony plantings.)

First, get to know the plants you adore by studying up on them and then growing

I grew up in the era of suburban foundation plantings—juniper, yew, and arborvitae flanking the front and side of almost every house in the neighborhood, with the occasional hosta or hydrangea thrown in. Yards were stretches of lawn dotted with little maple trees (the same trees that now obscure the houses), and gardens were boxed-in areas of the backyard where vegetables grew. Flowers were planted either in soldierly lines in front of the foundation plants or in circular beds of annuals in the front yard. Small city gardens were often scaled-back versions of the same idea—tightly sheared hedges of privet, barberry, or boxwood brightened by containers of pansies or geraniums, with petunias or impatiens (we called them "Busy Lizzies") growing in window boxes. Scores of gifted gardeners were plying their craft in the fifties and sixties—I just didn't know it then.

As the baby boomers grew up and bought their own homes or condos, it suddenly became passé to have a yard that looked just like mom and dad's, and a new era in landscaping was born. Plant-lovers and propagators who had been gardening for years were plucked away from their pruning shears and placed on book jackets, becoming the new icons of a generation. Landscaping developed into a big business—it's hard to blink without seeing a new garden-related product appearing on shelves or in catalogs. So why do countless gardens still look the same as they did a generation ago?

I suspect familiarity is part of the problem—when confronted with a nursery full of trees and shrubs, it is less intimidating to stick to a few familiar names than to investigate new and unfamiliar plants and cultivars,

'Jay Darling' crab apple (Malus)

especially when the old standbys and the newer varieties cost about the same.

It takes a tremendous effort of time and money to grow a tree or shrub, and when competition is tough, nurseries grow what they know they can sell. For the most part, these are the "old faithfuls": plants like lilac, forsythia, crape myrtle, rhododendron—plants that have spectacular blooms and familiar cultivar names.

Flowering pears and crab apples grow in many areas, but unfortunately they are sold almost generically. There are hundreds and hundreds of crab apple cultivars, with different growth habits (tall and oval, short and round, weeping, spreading, shrubby) and different characteristics. Some have great flowers only every other year; some have fruit

that disappears before the leaves (taking away some of the ornamental value); others have brilliant and persistent fruit. Some cultivars are highly prone to disease, while others are highly disease resistant; some have autumn color; some are fragrant. But what do you see at the garden center? A label that says "pink flowering crab" or "white flowering crab." Many nurseries and mail-order catalogs are still selling older disease-prone cultivars, such as 'Hopa', even though far superior crab apples are available.

If you're looking for 'Purple Wave' petunias and you have to settle for a different type, it's only going to affect your garden design for a season. But if you get a tree that is substandard, prone to disease, messy, or just the wrong tree for the spot, one of two things will probably happen: it will either die and you'll have to start over again or it will live and you'll have to deal with the mess and disease for thirty years or so. When it comes to trees and shrubs that will take up a significant part of your landscape (and budget!), it pays to be demanding. As consumers become better educated about plants of all types, a revolution is slowly happening—catalogs are making more of an effort to show the true color of flowers (they are still often wrong), and sometimes they will even warn you about notoriously invasive plants such as lythrum (*Lythrum salicaria*) and loosestrife (*Lythrum virgatum*). As consumers demand the newer, more disease-resistant varieties and cultivars, more wholesale nurseries will grow them, so more catalogs and garden centers can buy them; prices will stay competitive so you can plant the trees that are *not* like those that were in your father's garden.

them. Before you start to plant, browse seed and plant catalogs, your favorite gardening magazines, and illustrated encyclopedias of plants to learn whether those English delphiniums you've been coveting will survive your cold winters (they probably won't). You might also consult local nursery growers or your Agricultural Extension Service for advice on whether a particular plant will grow in your area. In addition to considering your plant hardiness zone, you'll need to assess the conditions in your garden, including your soil type, whether you have adequate drainage, and whether your yard is mostly sunny or shady. If your indigenous soil is nutrient-poor or excessively acidic or alkaline, you can do a great deal to improve the overall conditions in your garden by amending and conditioning the soil, or adding raised beds to increase drainage. But there is no test like the stick-it-in-the-

garden test to see how a plant will really grow on your site.

Once you've established that you're not dooming the plant by placing it in an environment where it simply cannot survive, it's worth a bit of experimentation to see which are the best plants for your garden. If a color combination isn't pleasing or a plant is too finicky, change it or toss it—even crummy plants make great compost. The late Henry Mitchell, who for many years wrote a column called "Earthman" for the *Washington Post*, was one of my favorite garden writers because he was a little cranky, didn't mince words, and didn't say something was easy when it wasn't, or would work when it wouldn't. His advice for beginning gardeners was to get out there and plant some things, then decide whether you like the results or not, and learn from your mistakes: "There is, so far

as I can learn, no substitute for that process; though much wear and tear is saved by thinking first, and learning a little first." Since Mitchell's own Zone 6 garden was a small city lot, he felt strongly about people who overplanted these spaces with large shade trees, saying that many people "believe a little switch of a tree should be planted 10 feet (3m) from another little switch of a tree; and they believe this in spite of the evidence of 100-foot (30m) yellow poplars, oaks, and so forth all over the city. The average city lot might easily accommodate a dogwood, an ironwood, a persimmon, a crape myrtle, or something of that kind."

There are two important small garden precautions to remember: first, some plants are easier to put in than to take out. Be very cautious about planting anything described as "vigorous," "fast-growing," "spreading," or "invasive." Plant catalogs don't want to scare you off if they can help it, so if they say something is invasive, you had better believe it. Second, remember that if your garden is healthy, the plants in it are going to grow, getting bigger, wider, and sometimes taller. While a dwarf perennial may grow only 2 feet (60cm) tall, some so-called dwarf conifers are actually just slow growing, and may eventually reach 20 feet (6m)

LEFT: Native plants mix happily in a charming meadow planting. If this look is too wild for you, plant grasses and wildflowers in a well-defined bed surrounded by lawn. OPPOSITE: Roses sprawl over a picket fence in this cozy, cottage-style garden. There are many beautiful climbing roses to choose from, and they make excellent additions to small gardens.

tall. Hostas may start out as compact mounds but some can reach 2 feet (60cm) high by 4 feet (1.2m) wide. Many grasses and perennials can top 8 feet (2.4m). Unless you have a lot of time on your hands, continual pruning is not the best option; choose something that is going to grow into the space you want to fill and stay there.

If you aren't sure how big a tree, shrub, or flower will grow, visit a local arboretum or botanical garden to see a mature specimen—you may get a shock. The key to creating a small garden is easy: plant small and select plants that will stay small.

DESIGN CONSIDERATIONS

Before you begin to plan your garden, decide how you will use it. Do you want a garden that will be for your own privacy and pleasure or a more public front garden that the neighborhood can enjoy? Will your garden space be used more for entertaining or for quiet contemplation? Will children be playing in and around the garden or will it be mostly for the benefit of adults? Your answers to these questions will help you decide the best way to approach a garden plan.

A garden intended for repose is best delegated to the backyard, where you will be able to enjoy your space without the distraction of passing traffic. A tall hedge or a fence will allow you to create a spot that is even more secluded. See Chapter 3, Secret Spaces, for more ideas on planning gardens in enclosed areas or creating tranquil spots within a larger yard.

You can plant a garden that both you and your neighbors can enjoy in front of a

Pagoda dogwood (Cornus alternifolia)

Japanese maple (Acer palmatum 'Oshio-Beni')

Trees and large shrubs should be selected with care for gardens planted close to the house. Be sure to give them room to grow and spread—pruning should be done to remove suckers and deadwood, and to maintain the natural shape of the tree. Don't try to use pruning as a method for forcing a large plant into a small space; the tops of trees should *never* be chopped off. If there are overhanging roofs or electrical wires nearby, select a tree or shrub that will not exceed 20 feet (6m) in height. Weeping trees can get quite large depending on the variety, but often they add width rather than height. Many weepers will send up shoots from the grafting point; these should be pruned regularly to keep the tree from looking messy. Some weepers also need to be staked when young.

Dwarf conifers are available in blues, golds, and many shades of green, with soft or stiff needles and shapes and sizes to suit every need. Dwarf conifers often originate as witches'-brooms—very dense clusters of branches resembling birds' nests, which are often caused by insects or fungi. These are

true dwarfs, but many other so-called dwarfs are just very slow-growing trees; be careful not to confuse the two because the slow growers will eventually reach full size. The true dwarf conifers may sometimes send out a shoot or "leader" reverting to the natural form of the species; these should be pruned out to maintain the dwarf size of the plant.

There are many lovely shade trees but most get too big for city lots; even some suburban and country homes can be dwarfed by too-large trees. Mid-size trees—those that grow to 35 feet (10.5m) or less—are a better choice for small lots. For planting around a deck or patio, look for a tree such as a thornless honey locust that casts only filtered shade and has leaves that break up and blow away. Trees and shrubs like 'Winter King' hawthorn, flowering dogwood (*Cornus florida*), pagoda dogwood (*Cornus alternifolia*), and double file viburnum (*Viburnum plicatum* var. *tomentosum* 'Mariesii') all have strong horizontal branching that can add architectural interest to a small yard.

Other trees and shrubs have ornamental bark, providing invaluable interest to the garden in winter. Trees with ornamental bark include Westonbirt dogwood (*Cornus alba* 'Sibirica'), coralbark dogwood (*Cornus sericea* 'Cardinal'), coralbark maple (*Acer palmatum* 'Sango Kaku', syn. 'Senkaki'), paperbark maple (*Acer griseum*), lacebark pine (*Pinus bungeana*), river birch (*Betula nigra* 'Heritage'), peeling bark cherry (*Prunus serrulata* var. *tibetica*), and amur cherry (*Prunus maackii*).

Narrow, or fastigiate, forms of many trees are available, and these are particularly suitable for planting in smaller garden areas. Sourwood (*Oxydendrum arboreum*) is a narrow, upright tree that will reach a height of about

20 feet (6m) and a width of 13 feet (4m) in about twenty years; it also offers striking white flowers and brilliant autumn color. The Serbian spruce (*Picea omorika*) is an elegant, narrow-growing conifer, more suitable to small lots than other spruces. The ginkgo *Ginkgo biloba* 'Princeton Sentry', flowering pear *Pyrus calleryana* 'Capital', sugar maple *Acer saccharum* 'Endowment Columnar', Oriental cherry *Prunus serrulata* 'Amanogawa', flowering crab apple *Malus* 'Sentinel', and the English oak *Quercus robur* forma *fastigiata* 'Skyrocket' are all narrowly columnar trees suitable for planting relatively close to the house. Other small ornamental trees to consider include Eastern redbud (*Cercis canadensis*), Chinese redbud (*Cercis chinensis*), kousa dogwood (*Cornus kousa*), apple serviceberry (*Amelanchier grandiflora*), Japanese maple (*Acer palmatum* cultivars), full-moon maple (*Acer japonicum*), amur maple (*Acer ginnala*), red horse chestnut (*Aesculus carnea* 'Briotii'), small crab apples (such as *Malus* × 'Satin Cloud'), Japanese snowbell (*Styrax japonicus*), and stewartia (*Stewartia pseudocamellia*).

city lot, on a street-facing balcony, around a front porch, or curved around the front yard. The type of garden you choose will depend largely on your tastes and somewhat on the architecture of your house. A rigidly planted formal garden may look jarring in front of a quaint cottage, just as unmowed tall prairie grasses will seem unkempt on the lawn of a Georgian mansion. Consider the style of your house and think of your garden as an extension of that style.

Many houses, particularly newer ones, are not built to a specific architectural style and are well suited to any number of garden styles. You can get the best of both formal and informal garden style if you maintain strict, geometric beds that are planted with a riot of old-fashioned flowers. If you plan to create a nontraditional garden, make sure there are no ordinances to prohibit it—municipalities are sometimes slow to catch up on landscaping trends such

as meadow plantings, and other communities restrict the installation of walls, fences, and other garden structures.

This island bed creates a pleasing view from the patio and offers an unobtrusive partial screen. In addition, the small bed confines the planting to an easily manageable space. In a bed as compact as this one, it is possible to plant and replant throughout the season so that the garden is always in full bloom.

Ornamental grasses bring a distinctive style to any garden with their beautiful architectural forms and subtle colors. While there is no hard and fast rule for working with grasses, they do seem to lend themselves best to dramatic designs. In late summer, as the sun begins to drop, there is nothing quite so breathtaking as long sweeps of tall grasses billowing against the brilliant sky. Even in the dead of winter, when ornamental grasses become frozen fountains, their presence keeps the garden alive. Grasses can be used as specimens, edging plants, elements in Japanese gardens, container plants, and, massed together, as a thematic design all their own. They work especially well in combination with yellow, gold, rust, and bronze perennials or chrysanthemums.

Easy to grow and maintain, most grasses are relatively disease-and pest-free. Spring is the best time to plant, cut back, and (when necessary) divide ornamental grasses. Before planting an ornamental grass, though, learn a bit about it—that sweet little grass in the container could quickly become a towering 8-foot (2.4m) giant. A running grass that spreads by aboveground stolons or underground rhizomes may become invasive—a serious problem if your space is limited—so look for clump-forming grasses instead. Some ornamental grasses thrive in hot, dry conditions; others require constant moisture and some shade to survive. A severe winter will wipe out certain species, while others will spread under your driveway and pop up across the street.

The following list will acquaint you with some ornamental grasses that are well suited for small gardens.

BLUE OAT GRASS (*Helictotrichon sempervirens*) Blue oat grass is slightly taller and more arching than the fescues; reaching 12 to 18 inches (30 to 45cm), it is an attractive plant for the front of a perennial border.

DWARF PAMPAS GRASS (*Cortaderia selloana* 'Pumila') Slightly hardier than common pampas grass, dwarf pampas grass is much more suitable for the average-size garden (it does not reseed itself and so is an excellent choice for gardens with limited space). This cultivar should bloom the first year, with 3 to 5 flower spikes by late summer. If you live in the South

Dwarf pampas grass (**Cortaderia selloana** '**Pumila**')

'Silbersee' fescue (**Festuca valesiaca** '**Silbersee**')

Japanese silver grass (**Miscanthus sinensis**)

and prefer to make a statement with the more tender full-size pampas grass, be sure to purchase one of the new cultivars, such as pink-plumed 'Rosea' or heavy-flowering 'Sunningdale Silver', which are preferable to the species.

FESCUES (*Festuca* spp.) Several species of this compact blue-gray grass are highly ornamental and are widely used as accent plants; most are relatively hardy and heat-tolerant. 'Elijah Blue' blue-silver fescue makes a neatly rounded edging plant, and grows only 8 inches (20cm) tall.

FOUNTAIN GRASS (*Pennisetum alopecuroides*) This species, which grows 2 to 3 feet (60 to 90cm) tall and as wide, is often planted in large drifts behind sweeps of rudbeckias and lower-growing grasses. It's also a great grass for the back of the flower border and along the foundations of houses. The cultivars 'Hameln' and 'Little Bunny' have a similar form but are more compact.

GOLDEN VARIEGATED HAKONE GRASS (*Hakonechloa macra* 'Aureola') With striking white-and-gold coloration, this gracefully arching plant looks as if it has been bent over by strong winds. It needs moisture: the hotter the summer, the more shade it requires. Foliage turns pink-red in autumn.

JAPANESE SILVER GRASS (*Miscanthus sinensis*) There are many beautiful specimen plants in this species, and most are relatively trouble-free. This grass is excellent at the back of a border or planted as a screen. It will also grow in shallow water or along a pond or stream. Among the best Japanese silver grasses are the cultivars 'Morning Light', 'Silberfeder', 'Gracillimus', 'Stricta', and the variety *purpurascens*.

RATTLESNAKE GRASS (*Briza media*) Rattlesnake grass grows to a modest size and looks good both as a specimen and planted in large groups. It does best in full sun but should not be allowed to dry out; it is hardy throughout much of North America.

'RED BARON' BLOOD GRASS (*Imperata cylindrica* 'Red Baron') This 1½-foot-tall (45cm) grass has unforgettable red foliage, but is related to grasses so invasive that they have been banned in some parts of North America. This cultivar is a small, slow-spreading ornamental, but may occasionally revert to its aggressive ancestor. If your 'Red Baron' blood grass mutates to a nonred form, remove it from your garden right away. To enjoy this attractive grass without fear, you may prefer to plant it in a container.

REED GRASSES (*Calamagrostis* spp.) Several species and hybrids (feather reed grass, foxtail grass, variegated reed grass) are suitable for the garden. A relatively hardy grass, it should be planted in shade where summers are hot.

SEDGE (*Carex stricta* 'Bowles Golden') This pretty yellow-green grass pops up in many English garden books. Gardeners in cold areas may not find it hardy enough for winter. Where summers are hot this grass needs regular moisture and some shade.

One cautionary note—feather grass (*Stipa* spp.) may look nice, but the needlelike fibers of its bristly flowers can cause painful damage to dogs who venture too close. Also, this genus goes dormant in summer and is considered a fire hazard in some areas.

'Stricta' reed grass (**Calamagrostis acutiflora** *'Stricta'*)

If children will be using the garden, you may want to exclude plants that could be dangerous, or at least keep those plants away from traffic areas. Avoid using shrubs and trees with thorns, such as roses, barberry, pyracantha, quince, hawthorn, and many locusts; plants that attract large numbers of bees, such as linden, orange jasmine, mint, and many flowers; plants that can irritate sensitive skin, such as alstroemeria, daphne, dictamnus, euphorbia, German primula, and rue; and plants that are poisonous if eaten, such as monkshood, horse chestnut, columbine, deadly nightshade, angel's trumpet, colchicum, lily-of-the-valley, delphinium, laburnum, lantana, yew, hellebores, glory lily, lupines, and cherry laurel.

FRAME YOUR GARDEN

In a small garden, everything is brought into sharp focus, as if a camera lens had suddenly zoomed in and framed it in a photograph. Large gardens may have a more extravagant variety of plants and room for massive trees, but they tend to lose some impact because there is too much to take in all at once. Working within the boundaries of a small yard, without the dis-

Defined by the house on one side and gentle hills on the other, this tiny sloping garden becomes a showcase for a gallery of spring-blooming bulbs, including hyacinths, tulips, daffodils, and grape hyacinths. The immediacy of a small garden lends itself well to this patchwork style of planting, since every flower can be seen and appreciated. Vast areas, on the other hand, have more visual impact when planted with sweeps of a single type of bulb.

tractions of distant features, each plant and garden feature becomes more prominent .

Look out your window or doorway, off into the distance—do you see hills, mountains, treetops? If so, try to frame these vistas when planning your garden. If, like many of us, your view leaves something to be desired or the horizon is flat as a pancake, see if there is an interesting backdrop you can "borrow"—a neighbor's weeping cherry, a stand of large pines, the rough brick of the building next door, a decorative fence, or even an old farmhouse in the distance. An illusion of depth is created by framing distant features with trees or shrubs, making the garden appear larger.

Another optical illusion involves making use of advancing and receding colors. "Hot colors"—such as red, orange, and bright yellow—seem to leap forward, and are best planted in the foreground. Pastels, on the other hand, especially blues and pale violets, create an illusion of distance. Plant flowers with these colors at the back of the garden to increase the feeling of depth.

You might also use a garden accent to increase the visual distance in your yard. An urn, a sculpture, a birdbath, or some other decorative object placed at the end of a long, narrow path draws the eye forward to the ornament, creating an illusion of distance. Interesting plantings or smaller ornaments placed on either side of the path will encourage attention to rest briefly on each before finishing at the focal point at the end of the walkway. The additional time it takes the eye to travel to the end of the path furthers the illusion of depth.

GARDEN ROOMS

Another popular approach to designing small, and even large, gardens is to think of the space as an outdoor "room" or a series of rooms. Each section of the garden has its allotted space and use. You might create an area for alfresco dining, a space for the kids to play, or a leafy bower with a bench.

If your garden is extremely small you might only have space for one room with attendant plantings. You'll have to decide which of the many possible functions is most important to you. Give the same thought and care to decorating your garden room that you would to an interior space. Consider movement, texture, color, and balance between all the elements, organic and inorganic alike.

A garden ornament or two can add a feeling of comfort and individuality, and may serve a practical purpose as well. A well-placed mirror can expand the view by reflecting the garden scene. Birdhouses and butterfly shelters can be highly decorative and help draw these lovely and useful winged creatures to your garden. Ornamental planters allow you to grow plants you might not otherwise have space for and let you introduce color and pattern in creative ways.

Make sure that any furniture used in your garden room is in keeping with the garden style and that it can withstand the ravages of cold and wet weather. Iron, cast-aluminum, treated or painted wood, and even plastic pieces are appropriate in garden settings. A table and chairs are the best option for an area where you plan to eat or

(continued on page 24)

Hostas are the hottest choice for shady spots in the garden, and with good reason. Hundreds of hostas line the pages of mail-order catalogs, displaying an amazing variety of form, foliage, color, size, and sun-tolerance. Easy to grow, simple to maintain, and bothered by very few pests or diseases (slugs are the slimy exception), hostas are just about foolproof. If there is one mistake that novice gardeners make with hostas, it is planting them in too much sun. Hostas were literally "made in the shade"—too much sun will cause the foliage to wither, fade, and burn.

Choosing a hosta is the hard part, because photographs in books, magazines, and catalogs make every one look so beautiful and tempting. In the pictures, hostas fill undulating beds and gracefully spill out of containers; tiny fingers of variegated hostas line paths beside grooved and seersucker leaves, forming an understory for blue hostas the size of elephant ears. It would take an artist's palette to illustrate all the shades of blue, green, gold, cream, and ivory that hosta leaves encompass, and you'd need several more shades to capture the flowers, which rise above the leaves in lavender or white and in varying sizes and fragrances. Without rubbing the thick texture of the leaves between your fingers, without experiencing the delicate fragrance or subtle blends of color, how does an average gardener (who doesn't have deep pockets or acres of land) know which hostas to choose?

One way is to look at what everyone else is buying. Among the best-selling hostas reported by the Perennial Plant Association are *Hosta albomarginata*, *H. sieboldiana* 'Elegans', 'Francee', 'Royal Standard', 'Frances Williams', 'Halcyon', 'Sum and Substance',

'Fragrant Bouquet' hosta, foreground; 'Blue Angel' hosta, background.

'Krossa Regal', 'Gold Standard', 'August Moon', and 'Patriot'. But best-sellers are not necessarily the *favorites* of either the wholesalers or their customers. One hosta specialist notes, "We sell out of every hosta we carry, so the best-sellers are just the ones that we can get." Limited availability of some hostas may create high prices initially, as with 'Patriot' (a sport of the popular 'Francee'), but as availability increases, prices drop. The American Hosta Society publishes its members' top 10 favorite hostas each year; for 1995, these were, in order of preference: 'Sum and Substance'; 'Gold Standard'; 'Great Expectations'; *H. montana* 'Aureomarginata'; *H. fluctuans* 'Variegated'; 'Frances Williams'; 'Krossa Regal'; *H. tokudama* 'Aureonebulosa'; 'Love Pat'; and 'Francee'. Hosta specialists like the

scent of 'So Sweet', 'Fragrant Bouquet', and 'Summer Fragrance'; the sun-tolerance of 'Golden Tiara' and *H. undulata* 'Variegata'; the form of *H. fluctuans* 'Variegated'; the randomly variegated foliage of 'Middle Ridge'; the large white flowers of *H. plantaginea*; the texture of 'Green Sheen' and 'Leather Sheen'; and the extremely large size of *H. nigrescens* 'Elatior'.

Whatever your garden needs, you'll be able to find a hosta that will suit. Browse through the following lists to find one that appeals, and then plop it in and watch it grow.

TEENY, TINY, AND TOT-SIZED HOSTAS (UNDER 18" [45CM] TALL)

'Allan P. McConnell' (12″ T/32″ W [30/81cm])
 Medium green leaves with white margins
'Brim Cup' (12″ T/24″ W [30/60cm])
 Seersucker leaves with white margins
'Chartreuse Wiggles' (6″ T/9″ W [15/23cm])
 Long, narrow, lance-shaped leaves
'Dorset Blue' (8″ T/12″ W [20/30cm])
 Round blue leaves; white flowers
'Emerald Skies' (6″ T/16″ W [15/40.5cm])
 Shiny dark green leaves; white flowers
'Fragrant Gold' (14″ T/38″ W [35.5/96.5cm])
 Sun-tolerant gold leaves; fragrant flowers
'Ginko Craig' (15″ T/36″ W [38/90cm])
 Neatly mounded habit; narrow leaves
'Gold Edger' (12″ T/45″ W [30/114cm])
 Heavy-flowering gold hosta; good for partial sun
'Golden Tiara' (16″ T/40″ W [40.5/101.5cm])
 Green-and-yellow variegated foliage
H. pulchella 'Kifukurin' (4″ T/8″ W [10/20cm])
 Glossy dark green leaves with yellow edge
H. venusta 'Variegata' (5″ T/8″ W [13/20cm])
 Cream and green variegated foliage
'Janet' (16″ T/45″ W [40.5/114cm]) Green margin, chartreuse to white variegation

'Just So' (6″ T/10″ W [15/25.5cm]) Tiny leaves combining yellow, gold, and green

'Kabitan' (10″ T/15″ W [25.5/38cm]) Narrow, wavy green margins, chartreuse center

'Leather Sheen' (15″ T/30″ W [38/75cm]) Glossy leaves with heavy texture

'Little Aurora' (8″ T/12″ W [15/30cm]) Puckered, metallic gold leaves

'Middle Ridge' (16″ T/28″ W [40.5/71cm]) Wavy leaves with streaky white center

'Northern Lights' (16″ T/30″ W [40.5/75cm]) Award winner; variegated mutation of 'Elegans'

'Patriot' (12″ T/30″ W [30/75cm]) Award winner; dark green leaves with wide white edge

'Peace' (12″ T/20″ W [30/51cm]) Blue-green leaves with variegated margins

'Shining Tot' (4″ T/13″ W [10/33cm]) Dark green foliage

'Sitting Pretty' (5″ T/8″ W [13/20cm]) Lance-shaped, variegated leaves

'Stiletto' (8″ T/12″ W [20/30cm]) Masses of gold-edged, lance-shaped leaves

'Summer Music' (15″ T/24″ W [38/60cm]) Unusual white center, green/gold edge

MEDIUM TO LARGE HOSTAS (18″–25″ [45–63.5CM] TALL)

'August Moon' (20″ T/30″ W [51/75cm]) Yellow/green foliage; white flowers

'Aurora Borealis' (24″ T/66″ W [60/167.5cm]) Rounded green leaves with gold margins

'Blue Seer' (25″ T/60″ W [63.5/152.5cm]) Heavily textured blue leaves; white flowers

'Blue Wedgwood' (18″ T/38″ W [45/96.5cm]) Heart-shaped blue leaves

'Christmas Tree' (20″ T/36″ W [51/90cm]) 'Frances Williams' hybrid; narrow white margin

'Fragrant Bouquet' (18″ T/26″ W [45/66cm]) Variegated foliage; fragrant white flowers

'Francee' (26″ T/60″ W [66/152.5cm]) One of the best variegated hostas

'Geisha' (22″ T/45″ W [56/114cm]) Very glossy, dark green, edged leaves, chartreuse center

'Gold Standard' (24″ T/60″ W [60/152.5cm]) Popular gold/green variegated hosta

'Great Expectations' (22″ T/30″ W [56/75cm]) Wide, irregular variegation, white flowers

'Hadspen Blue' (18″ T/50″ W [45/127cm]) Deep blue foliage

'Halcyon' (18″ T/40″ W [45/101.5cm]) Neat clump of heavy blue leaves

H. plantaginea (24″ T/36″ W [60/90cm]) Very large, fragrant white flowers

H. tokudama 'Aureonebulosa' (18″ T/48″ W [45/120cm]) Beautifully colored foliage

H. ventricosa 'Aureomarginata' (24″ T/50″ W [60/127cm]) Attractive, irregular variegation

'Love Pat' (22″ T/48″ W [59/120cm]) Textured blue foliage; sun-tolerant

'Maekawa' (20″ T/32″ W [51/81cm]) Gray/green ridged leaves with silvery white underside

'Royal Standard' (24″ T/40″ W [60/101.5cm]) Classic green foliage and white flowers

'Shade Fanfare' (25″ T/54″ W [63.5/137cm]) Award winner; textured, variegated leaves

'So Sweet' (18″ T/36″ W [45/90cm]) Variegated leaves; very fragrant white flowers

'Sun Power' (26″ T/50″ W [66/127cm]) Gold foliage; excellent planted with blue hostas

'Wide Brim' (18″ T/45″ W [45/114cm]) Award winner; blue-green foliage with cream edge

'Zounds' (26″ T/48″ W [66/120cm]) Attractive golden leaves

REALLY BIG ONES (MORE THAN 30″ [75CM] TALL)

'Big Daddy' (36″ T/48″ W [90/120cm]) Blue-green leaves; white flowers

'Blue Angel' (48″ T/65″ W [120/165cm]) Award winner; blue foliage; white flowers

'Blue Mammoth' (45″ T/70″ W [114/178cm]) One of the largest hostas

'Color Glory' (36″ T/40″ W [90/101.5cm]) Wide leaves with yellow centers

'Frances Williams' (32″ T/40″ W [81/101.5cm]) A classic; chartreuse-edged blue/green leaves

'Green Sheen' (32″ T/48″ W [81/120cm]) Medium green foliage with heavy substance

H. fluctuans 'Variegated' (36″ T/60″ W [90/152.5cm])—Blue-green leaves with cream/gold edge

H. montana 'Aureomarginata' (42″ T/64″ W [106.5/162.5cm])—Glossy green, variegated leaves

H. nigrescens 'Elatior' (30″ T/40″ W [75/101.5cm])—Shiny light green foliage

H. sieboldiana 'Elegans' (38″ T/60″ W [96.5/152.5cm])—One of the most popular "big blues"

'Krossa Regal' (30″ T/54″ W [75/137cm])—Heavy blue-gray leaves

'Solar Flare' (30″ T/42″ W [75/106.5cm])—Heart-shaped, textured gold leaves

'Sum and Substance' (30″ T/64″ W [75/162.5cm])—Heavily textured chartreuse to gold leaves

work, but a bench, Adirondack chair, or small garden seat might be sufficient if you opt for a garden room with a contemplative flair.

If you have space for more than one room, you might segment them with an arbor, hedge, or a small gate. Or the divisions may be more subtle, created by a path, an area of lawn or paving, an arrangement of furniture, or a change in level.

Add layers and textures to your garden room by underplanting one or two small trees with a combination of perennials and low-growing shrubs. Colorful, fast-growing annuals such as 'Lavender Lady' globe ama-

ranth, 'Strawberry Cooler' periwinkles, and 'Pink Wave' petunias, can be used to fill in bare spots or to draw attention to a bench or garden ornament. Side yards that are often dry and shaded by the house can be used to draw visitors to a back garden. Create a winding path of brick, stone, or even shredded bark mulch, leaving as much space as possible between the walk and the house. Plant broad sweeps of low-maintenance perennials next to the house or, if the space isn't too narrow, you may want to try some small shrubs. If your side yard is sunny, plant drought-tolerant ornamental grasses,

daylilies, yucca, hybrid black-eyed Susans (*Rudbeckia* spp.), or small mounds of *Stephanandra incisa* 'Crispa'.

If the side yard is shady, combine hostas of different colors, sizes, and textures with ferns. Water well after planting, then add mulch to help retain moisture. The old-fashioned shrub *Hydrangea arborescens* 'Annabelle' has a loose, sprawling form and huge flowers; it adds interest to a side yard and is tolerant of both sun and shade as well as most soil types. Easy-care annuals such as impatiens can be tucked in a shady border to add color, while a medium- to large-size shrub, such as *Viburnum burkwood* 'Mohawk', placed at the end of the side garden will block the view to the backyard, adding a touch of mystery that pulls visitors down the garden path.

However you construct your garden room, remember to plant small, keeping the garden in balance with the architectural features of the building. By turning usable outdoor spaces into garden rooms, the boundaries between house and garden are softened and diminished until one flows naturally into the other.

Side yards offer special challenges because they are generally long and narrow, a shape that can be somewhat awkward. Here, the length of the yard is accentuated with a straight path. Note, though, that the path is off-center, a more imaginative way of laying out the space. It's also a design that allows for maximum width of one of the planting spaces. Tulips and rhododendrons lead the way with a burst of color, while well-tended shrubs lend year-round interest.

Garden Plan: A Sunny Summer Garden

Perennial gardens usually have a peak season of beauty when most of the flowers are in bloom; this full-sun garden will hit its stride midsummer and keep on getting better into early autumn. Customize this plan by using some of your personal favorites, working in other perennials that flower in late summer or using chrysanthemums to fill in any bare spots that may develop. The tall grasses and bright yellows make a bold effect that is softened by the cooling blue and purple tones.

Plant this garden against a back fence or a garage wall where you can see it from a window. You can also adapt it for a raised berm, offering a two-sided view by repeating the plants on both sides. Cut back the perennials when they have passed their prime but let the grasses become frozen fountains in the winter, cutting the dead foliage away in early spring. Water well until the plants are established; in future years this bed should require a minimal amount of supplemental watering.

PLANT LIST

1. 'Morning Light' Japanese silver grass (*Miscanthus sinensis* 'Morning Light')
2. Giant sunflower (*Helianthus giganteus*) (8-10′ [2.4–3m] tall)
3. 'Goldgreenheart' oxeye (*Heliopsis* 'Goldgreenheart')
4. False indigo (*Baptisia australis*)
5. 'Blue Wonder' catmint (*Nepeta × faassenii* 'Blue Wonder')
6. 'Hameln' Chinese pennisetum (*Pennisetum alopecuroides* 'Hameln')
7. 'Happy Returns' daylily (*Hemerocallis ×* 'Happy Returns')

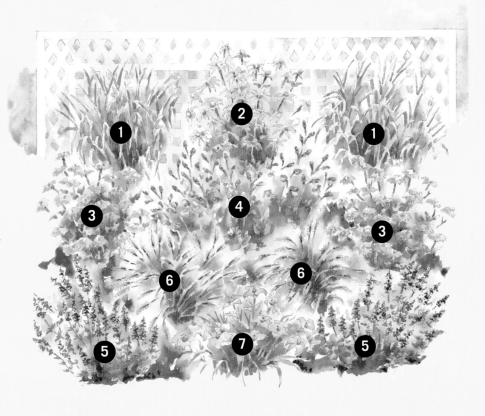

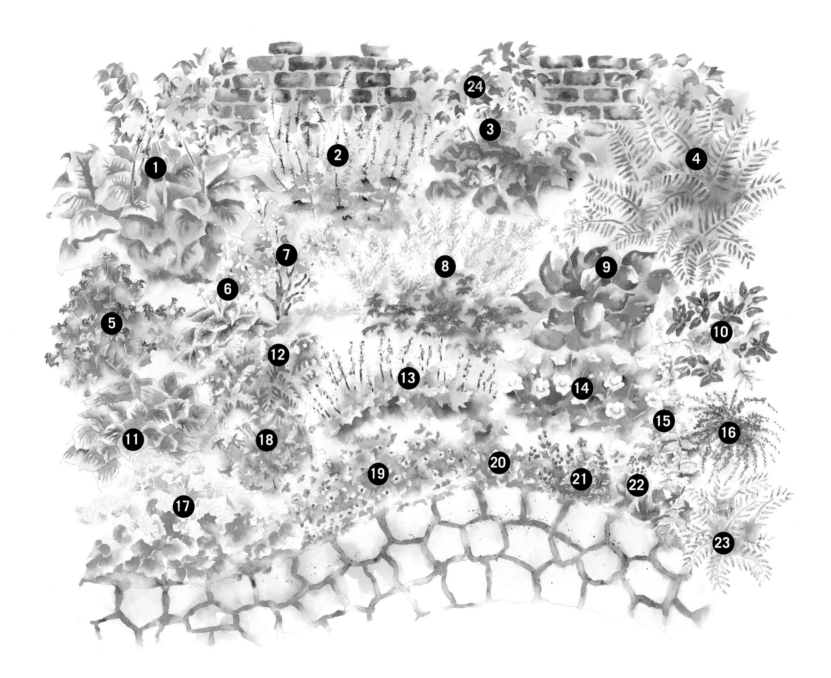

Garden Plan: A Shady Garden for Foliage and Color

There is no reason to let shady spots become a wasteland of spotty lawn or a boring strip of generic, variegated hostas. A large number of plants thrive in partial or even full shade, with enough variety of foliage and flower to excite any garden lover. Since strong color will not be a feature in this shade garden, I have included a number of perennials whose subtle coloring and distinctive foliage will provide the attraction. Late spring and early summer will be the peak season for this garden in most regions, but an underplanting of bulbs can stretch it even further.

Try this garden in a walled courtyard, a narrow city garden, or along the side of a house in suburbia. Because shrubs and large hostas are included, this garden is not tiny in itself, but it contains a number of features that make the most of a restricted space. Plants that grow in layers combined with different levels of plants—from groundcovers to small trees—add perspective; this effect can be heightened by planting a fence, wall, or garage behind the garden with a climber like 'Robusta' Boston ivy (*Parthenocissus tricuspidata* 'Robusta'), which will add height and brilliant red autumn color. Apply a natural-looking mulch after planting and keep well-watered until the plants are established.

PLANT LIST

*Shrubs and perennials along a path
of mulch, gravel, flagstone, or brick*

1. 'Sum and Substance' hosta (*Hosta* 'Sum and Substance')
2. 'Lavender Mist' meadow rue (*Thalictrum rochebrunianum* 'Lavender Mist')
3. Yellow waxbells (*Kirengeshoma palmata*)
4. Ostrich fern (*Matteuccia struthiopteris*)
5. Masterwort (*Astrantia rosea*)
6. 'Frances Williams' hosta (*Hosta sieboldiana* 'Frances Williams')
7. 'Forest Prince' serviceberry (*Amelanchier* 'Forest Prince')
8. 'Peach Blossom' astilbe (*Astilbe* × *rosea* 'Peach Blossom')
9. 'Aureonebulosa' hosta (*Hosta tokudama* 'Aureonebulosa')
10. 'Royal Purple' smoke tree (*Cotinus coggygria* 'Royal Purple')
11. 'Halcyon' hosta (*Hosta* 'Halcyon')
12. 'Snowdrift' bleeding heart (*Dicentra* × 'Snowdrift')
13. Foamflower (*Tiarella cordifolia*)
14. 'Honorine Jobert' anemone (*Anemone* × 'Honorine Jobert')
15. 'White Nancy' lamium (*Lamium* 'White Nancy')
16. 'Crispa' lace shrub (*Stephanandra incisa* 'Crispa')
17. Lady's-mantle (*Alchemilla mollis*)
18. Wild columbine (*Aquilegia canadensis*)
19. 'Ralph Shugert' common periwinkle (*Vinca minor* 'Ralph Shugert')
20. Wild ginger (*Asarum europaeum*)
21. 'Mrs. Moon' lungwort (*Pulmonaria saccharata* 'Mrs. Moon')
22. Bergenia (*Bergenia cordifolia*)
23. 'Pictum' Japanese painted fern (*Athyrium nipponicum* 'Pictum')
24. 'Robusta' Boston ivy (*Parthenocissus tricuspidata* 'Robusta')—planted along a house, wall, or fence

Underplanting the shrubs and perennials with bulbs, most of which flower early in the year, will greatly extend the bloom season in your garden. Following is a list of bulbs that I suggest planting beneath the plants shown in the plan.

- Underplant 17 with 'Ehrlicheer' daffodil
- Underplant 23 with 'Thalia' narcissus
- Underplant 12 and 14 with Virginia bluebells (*Mertensia virginica*)
- Underplant 19 with glory-of-the-snow (*Chionodoxa luciliae*)
- Underplant 22 with Spanish bluebells (*Hyacinthoides hispanica*)
- Underplant 6, 9, and 11 with striped squill (*Puschkinia scilloides*)
- Underplant 10 with 'Petrel' narcissus
- Underplant 21 with 'Violet Queen' crocus
- Underplant 20 with common snowdrops (*Galanthus nivalis*)
- Underplant 13 with 'Lilac Perfection' peony-flowered tulip

Chapter 2

Gardens Above the Ground

WINDOW BOXES AND CONTAINER GARDENS

ABOVE: Common purple petunias become window box aristocrats when joined with silvery licorice plant, rosy verbena, and the tiny purple and white flowers of Lobelia erinus.
OPPOSITE: Lush greenery gives this city skyline a touch of the country—rooftop gardens provide city residents with a much-needed oasis.

Containers are not just for summer—this wooden barrel planted with 'Mount Hood' narcissus and trailing ivy makes a bold spring statement. Because the area is so small, it will be a simple matter to dig up spent bulbs and replant the container with later-season flowers.

of place on the steps of a bungalow, while inexpensive plastic pots would be incongruous on the porch of a plantation-style southern home. That is not to say that either of these couldn't be used if the owner really liked them, but the arrangement would probably end up looking off-key.

Plastic pots are actually preferable to terra-cotta for plants that need to stay moist, but terra-cotta pots are classics, and especially older ones (or pots made to look old) add a certain style to any container arrangement. Even the cheapest terra-cotta pots look nice as they are, although many artistic gardeners paint or decoupage them for added interest. Stone containers are available in both modern and classic styles— these have the benefit of usually getting through the winter undamaged, which is just as well since they are pretty near impossible to move. Unfortunately, they aren't absolutely guaranteed to make it through the winter and since they are quite expensive, many gardeners keep their stone planters on wheeled bases to facilitate moving them indoors for winter.

DESIGN BASICS

To make the most of a container arrangement, use a combination of plant shapes and sizes, remembering that large plants and

(*continued on page 34*)

T
o a gardener covered in clay, fresh from a muddy garden, the idea of gardening above the ground with soil confined to containers can seem mighty attractive. No digging, no weeding, no back-breaking labor—container planting sounds idyllic. The truth must be told, though— even gardening above the ground is painstaking, messy work that requires as much or more planning than a garden planted in the ground. Plants in window boxes, hanging baskets, and pots are entirely dependent

upon the gardener to provide sufficient water and nutrients to keep them alive.

THE CONTAINER

Gardening in containers is special since the containers can be as integral to the garden design as the plants inside them. The type of container you select depends on budget, taste, availability, and many other factors, but it should tie in with the architecture of the house and any surrounding structures. Elaborate Italian stone pots may look out

'Maori Sunrise' mountain flax (Phormium colensoi *'Maori Sunrise'*) *and* Scaevola aemula *'New Blue Wonder'*
are attractive and unusual plants worthy of a second look, and both grow well in the potted garden.
Classic terra-cotta pots are inexpensive, easy to find, and match well with every garden decor. In addition,
terra-cotta is ideal as a "background" container: you never need worry about it upstaging its contents
and it looks good mixed with almost any other type of container.

The great thing about containers is that they are perfect places to experiment with plants. If the combination doesn't thrive in one spot, try moving the container someplace else. If a plant doesn't look quite right, pull it out and pop it into another container.

There are other advantages to planting in containers. For instance, you may want to try a butterfly garden, an all-white garden, a hot color garden, or some other theme. Before going to the work and expense of planting a large bed, try out your ideas on a smaller scale first—in containers. If a plant has piqued your curiosity but you aren't quite sure how to fit it in your garden, start it in a container and get

A terra-cotta chimney pot with openings like those of a strawberry jar is planted with white and coral-colored lewisias.

This ususual potted garden features a bay tree and ferns.

to know it first. Containers are like cocktail parties—entertaining and not too much work.

Gardeners have one distinct advantage over painters: they can work on several planes. A dwarf tree, standard rose, or topiary planted in a container will add several feet in height to the gardener's visual canvas. Creeping, climbing, or vining plants, too, add unusual dimensions, whether foliage and flowers spill from hanging baskets or trail over the sides of earthbound containers. Decorative pots of different sizes, artfully arranged and handsomely planted, can become the focus of the whole garden.

Whatever plants you select, remember that they will not thrive unless they are planted in

well-drained soil (or a soilless mix), fertilized adequately, and watered regularly. Deadhead flowers to encourage repeat blooming, and experiment with different levels of light and shade if the plants seem overly stressed.

Following are some suggestions for interesting container combinations.

TRY CLEMATIS IN CONTAINERS Look for compact, heavy-flowering forms, particularly those that flower early in the season (about May or June). The clematis cultivar 'Snow Queen' is a compact grower that has received top awards at the Chelsea Flower Show in England. Other cultivars recommended for containers are 'Royalty', 'Pink Champagne', 'Mrs. P.B. Truax', 'Sunset', 'Arctic Queen', 'Silver Moon', and 'Fireworks'. Once the flowers finish, many clematis have interesting seedheads that will keep the container looking good.

A wooden barrel or a large clay pot is an excellent container choice for clematis. Train the vine on a sturdy support, and realize that it may take two to three years for the clematis to climb a 5-foot (1.5m) support. Place the container where it will get some protection from the sun and plan on moving it to a sheltered place such as a garage in the winter. Underplant the clematis with a small-leafed creeper such as 'Limelight' helichrysum or a trailing vinca.

CREATE AN ELEGANT ARRANGEMENT Take several deep purple petunias and mix in *Lisianthus eustoma* of the same color; add a white-leafed caladium (*Caladium bicolor*) such as 'White Christmas' or 'June Bride'. Sprinkle in a few tiny purple violas, too.

FILL CONTAINERS WITH BULBS Use a low container to create a striking arrangement of Greigii hybrid tulips such as 'Red Riding Hood'. Pack a larger, deeper container with African lily (*Agapanthus africanus* 'Albus') for a stunning summer display of white flowers that grow nearly 4 feet (1.2m) tall. Lilies are always a knockout in containers—the blossoms on Japanese lily (*Lilium speciosum* 'Rubrum') are dainty but bountiful, while gold-banded lilies (*Lilium auratum*) 'Gigi' and 'Casa Blanca' are several inches across and very fragrant.

ADD HERBS TO POTS Whether you use herbs for cooking or just like the way they look, most are made to order for containers. Spreading herbs such as mint and marjoram can easily be kept within bounds in a container, while those like salad burnet spill gracefully over the edge. Plant an assortment of scented geraniums, basil, sage, and thyme—be sure to handle their leaves to release each distinct fragrance. Add edible flowers, such as French marigolds or nasturtiums, for color and to use in salads.

STRAWBERRY JARS AREN'T JUST FOR STRAWBERRIES
While strawberries are pretty all by themselves, strawberry jars—with their multiple small openings—can be adapted for many other plants, too. Place a trailing plant like an ivy geranium in the top opening and fill the others with alyssum, ivy, pansies, or lobelia. Or plant 'Homestead Purple' verbena in the main opening and add 'Limelight' helichrysum to the rest. For small planters, try an assortment of low-growing dianthus, thyme, or sedum.

BE DARING—TRY TROPICALS Bougainvillea, hibiscus, diervilla, and lantana aren't plants that you normally see growing in Kansas City, Toronto, or Boston. But these tropicals, as well as some other Mexican, Chilean, and South African plants, grow fast enough to look great in a container all summer. Just think of them as very expensive petunias.

FOCUS ON FOLIAGE Hostas, grasses, ivies, and other plants normally grown for their foliage can make excellent subjects for containers. Make sure the container is large enough to hold the plant at its mature size, or be prepared to transplant.

PLANT A FEW CONTAINERS FOR AUTUMN INTEREST
No garden seems complete without chrysanthemums, and containers are a good place to put them since many are not hardy. Add ornamental kale or blue oat grass for interest and be sure to include something you haven't tried before, such as 'Snowbank' boltonia (*Boltonia asteroides* 'Snowbank'), 'Margarete' anemone (*Anemone* × *hybrida* 'Margarete'), 'Brilliant' sneezeweed (*Helenium autumnale* 'Brilliant'), or 'White Pearl' bugbane (*Cimicifuga simplex* 'While Pearl').

Deep purple 'Queen of the Night' tulips are an inspired choice for a container. This box-type planter offers plenty of space for an effective display.

bulky containers will monopolize the scene unless they are balanced by an interesting selection of medium and small containers. Container gardening can be as simple as a single window box artistically arranged with complementary flowers and intriguing foliage, or it can be as complex as a multi-tiered garden that includes climbing plants, hanging baskets, and potted trees or standard shrubs, as well as containers overflowing with flowers. Hanging baskets can be planted singly or in groups placed at different heights; the most natural-looking baskets are lined wire baskets filled with soil, planted, and covered in sphagnum moss (the moss is actually packed between the wires). By selecting compact plants that have a mounding or dense habit and combining them with a few tall or spiky plants and trailing vines, the garden will appear full and lush.

Some hanging baskets come with holes on the sides (similiar to strawberry pots) to create a fuller, rounder effect. Often, moss-lined baskets can be purchased in wrought-iron stands that are designed to look like topiary.

To my mind the most effective containers are really packed—it doesn't matter if they are packed with bulbs or with masses of a single type of plant, or whether the scheme is monochromatic or filled with flowers of every color. The trick—and this takes practice—is to pack a container full enough to keep it interesting, but allow enough space between plants to keep the air circulating between them and to keep the plants from merging into an amorphous jumble of foliage and color where nothing stands out.

OPPOSITE: *An impressive container—like this classically inspired stone trough—requires only the simplest of plantings. An understated arrangement of boxwood, narcissus, and primroses complements the elegant design of the planter. LEFT: Handpainted terra-cotta pots mix with containers startling and sublime in this whimsical setting.* Dendranthemum, *ornamental cabbages, and ivies are among the autumn-blooming plants that adorn this corner of the garden.*

ABOVE LEFT: A single container—if it's unusual in itself or if it is beautifully planted—can become the focal point of a garden. This appealing ceramic pot is filled with phormium, salvia, stocks, anemones, pansies, and boronia.
ABOVE RIGHT: Since hanging baskets are often viewed from afar or from below, plant them with flowers that will cascade over the edges. This moss-lined hanging basket is packed with an artistic arrangement of petunias, **Convolvulus sabatius,** *blue marguerites, scaevola, and 'Elegante' geraniums.*

I like containers that are tiny and delicate as well as those that stand up and shout; what I don't want to see is one wimpy flower surrounded by dirt. Because newly planted containers are bound to show a lot of dirt, I like to include several plants that will fill in quickly, as well as a few vines or creepers that will trail down the sides. Spiky plants are traditional in containers, but many other plants can add height and structure—consider lilies, for instance. Lilies are breathtaking when in bloom, but before and afterward their stems just look like stems. Overplant a lily bulb with a variety of annuals; when the lily blooms you have a knockout display and afterward, the annuals should be full enough to hide the stem from view. Perennials in larger sizes are very satisfactory for containers, since most gallon (3.7l)-size perennials will bloom the same year. Mums and grasses are great to carry a container into autumn—if the annuals are past their prime, pull them out and replace them with these or other cool-season plants like asters or ornamental kale. Many foliage plants, such as licorice plant (*Helichrysum petiolare*) will look great right up until the first hard frost; some roses will bloom in autumn, too, and look great in containers.

When selecting plants, be careful not to put something top-heavy in a small pot; the rule of thumb is that the height of the plant should be no more than 1½ times the height of the container. Also, remember that each plant has its particular needs,

Shopping for plants should be the easiest aspect of gardening—it is without doubt the most tempting. After putting a lot of time into researching plants and finally coming up with a short list for your garden, it can be very frustrating to go from one garden center to the next, finding the same old plants at each one. As nurseries and garden centers realize that their customers are becoming better educated and more selective in what they are buying, a better selection of plants is gradually becoming available. However, unless you live near a specialty nursery or herb farm, mail order may be your best bet to obtain hard-to-find plants. See the source list (page 116) for a selection of well-known mail-order companies. In addition to these, there are many regional or lesser-known companies. Mail-order nurseries generally have an excellent reputation for delivering merchandise in good condition and guaranteeing replacement of plants that don't survive. You'll have to look long and hard to find a local garden store that will guarantee plant material for a full year at no extra cost.

You can order seeds, plugs, bulbs, and annual and perennial plants as well as shrubs and trees by mail. The main benefit of mail order is the unbelievably wide range of available plants compared to what you might find locally. Prices range from reasonable to outrageous but since catalogs usually sell out of plants before the end of the season, people are obviously willing to pay even the top prices.

Packing material varies, but mail-order companies generally ship bareroot plants, which arrive with no soil, or smallish plants in a minimum of soil. The first time I received an order that I had placed through the mail,

I looked in vain for plants—all I could find were plastic bags apparently filled with peat moss and nothing else. On closer inspection, I found roots and tubers in the bags, but I had little hope of anything growing from such a depressing start. Much to my amazement, nearly every bag produced a healthy plant. I am now sold on bareroot plants, whether they are perennials, trees, or shrubs, although I prefer my perennials larger to start with, if possible.

Open all boxes of plant material right away, whether you are going to plant them immediately or not. Bulbs and bags of bareroot plants can be temporarily stored in the crisper drawer of a refrigerator if weather or your schedule prevents you from planting them. (I once forgot that I had done this and came across the bags of plants weeks later. I planted them right away and didn't lose a single one.) Bareroot trees should be unpacked, unwrapped, and set in a bucket of water overnight before planting. Plants shipped in containers are more vulnerable and should be watered, kept in a sheltered area overnight, and planted before the heat of the day when there are no drying winds. Dull, overcast days are the best for setting out plants.

Before spending a lot of time and effort on plant labels for the garden, it might be a good idea to compare the plants you received to the description of the plants you ordered. For one thing, catalogs are notorious for displaying flowers with artificially enhanced colors that are nothing like the real thing. Both at local garden centers and mail-order nurseries, plant labels can sometimes get switched or the plants get mislabeled. What you get in the mail will probably not be in

flower, so you could be in for a surprise. Last year I ordered baby's breath—the plant is now 1 foot (30cm) high and bloomed in April with masses of delicate purple flowers; I still haven't positively identified it. I do know that the six little pots of blue-flowering *Veronica latifolia* 'Crater Lake', a plant that usually grows to 12 inches (30cm) tall, turned out to be *Veronica repens*, a creeping plant that rarely tops 4 inches (10cm) in height. With mail-order shopping, as with anything else, let the buyer beware.

Remember that bareroot plants are alive and need to be unpacked with care. It might not look like much, but with proper handling this bareroot plant has just as much chance of thriving as a container-grown plant.

whether it is planted in the ground or aboveground. Shade-loving plants like hostas will still need shade; sun-loving plants like roses will still need sun. Group plants by their requirements and decide your plant combinations from there. Window boxes, containers, and hanging baskets can become miniature shade gardens or butterfly gardens—the same principles apply, just on a smaller scale.

PLANTING YOUR CONTAINERS

Plants in the ground can absorb nutrients from the surrounding soil, as well as organic material from compost, mulch, and falling leaves. Plants in containers are usually not mulched and are often planted in nothing more than a soilless planting mixture. Ask twenty gardeners to describe their ideal recipe for a container planting mix and you will get twenty different answers. Some expert gardeners swear by soilless mixes, while others are equally determined that a soilless mix is not sufficient to support a growing plant. I look for commercial potting mixes blending peat and perlite or peat and vermiculite; other specially prepared potting soil mixes come with water-retaining polymers and starter fertilizers already added. There is, however, agreement on one point: don't dig soil out of the yard to fill your containers. This soil tends to be very heavy and most containerized plants do better with a lighter mix; don't forget that roots need air as much as they need nutrients and water.

Fill containers about half full of your chosen planting mix, arrange the plants

on top, then pack more of the planting mix around them. Do not fill the container all the way to the top, or it will overflow when watered.

Containers for rooftop gardens and balconies can be structurally dangerous if they are too heavy or placed incorrectly. Avoid very large, heavy containers or be prepared to get expert advice. One tip professionals give is to place chips or blocks of Styrofoam in the base of sturdy planters—air and water can flow through or around

ABOVE: Foliage in a variety of shapes, colors, and textures combines beautifully in this expansive window box. Remembering to include interesting foliage plants assures that the box will look attractive long before and after flowers bloom. LEFT: This wicker basket includes both herbs and flowers—parsley, chives, stocks, and lobelia. OPPOSITE: Heath, wintergreen, Japanese skimmia, ivies, and 'Northern Lights' kale create an inspiring winter scene. Lining your pots up stairsteps is an interesting way to add different height levels to your scheme—just make sure that there's enough room on the steps for easy passage.

the Styrofoam and the planter is much lighter than if it were filled only with soil or a soil-and-gravel mix.

Commercial time-release "starter" fertilizers are sufficient for most container plants, although all fertilizers should be used with caution. Used too soon or in too great a quantity, fertilizer can burn plants. Do not be overgenerous when adding drops of fertilizer to water in order to dilute it; a drop or two more than the directions indicate could be deadly to certain plants. Plant fertilizer stakes have worked for me; and while I also like foliar feeders, they can be high in nitrogen, encouraging lush, green leaves at the expense of flowers. Again, the formula and frequency of a fertilization schedule are subjects experts disagree on. Some insist that once a month during the growing season is sufficient, while others prefer fertilizing about every two weeks.

WATERING CONTAINER GARDENS

Don't rely on rainfall to keep containerized plants watered—if the pot is sheltered by an overhanging roof, the rain may never reach it. If it does rain, it is up to the gardener to ensure that the container has sufficient drainage to keep it from flooding. Terra-cotta pots act like wicks to water, causing the plants to dry out more quickly than they would in plastic pots. Polymers that hold water in the soil are useful but should be used with caution; in a heavy rainfall poly-mers can absorb so much water that the container overflows, spilling a messy brew of water, plants, soil, and polymer crystals like globs of muddy Jell-O. Use a container that has adequate drainage holes—if you have a beautiful china container that can't be drilled, place the plants in a separate container and layer them one inside the other. If you are watering plants from an inside faucet, make sure that the faucet is not hooked up to a water softener and that the water is neither very hot nor very cold.

CARE AND MAINTENANCE

Deadhead flowers regularly and remove debris from containers—dead flowers not only look unsightly, they create a setting that is ripe for disease, fungi, and insect infestation. Herbs in containers benefit from shearing or pinching back; if performed early in the season, this is also useful to encourage heavy flowering on chrysanthe-mums. And while containers don't need weeding like plant beds do, weeds crop up in them from time to time. A light layer of mulch (not too close to the crown of the plant) will hold in water and discourage weeds, but some light weeding may still be necessary until the plants fill in. If a con-tainer packed with several plants just doesn't look right, try moving it to a different loca-tion where there is more or less light, or shelter from the wind. If this doesn't solve the problem, decide if the whole container is unsatisfactory or if the problem is centered around one or two plants. The great thing about containers is that if something doesn't work you can pluck it out and try something else. Don't toss the offending plant—it may suddenly steal the show in another combi-nation planting.

Plants play second fiddle to structure in this geometrically appealing rooftop garden. With space for a table and chairs, buffet tables, or even a small dance floor, this garden is made for entertaining. Trees, shrubs, and perennials adorning the perimeter serve as privacy screens and help to create the illusion of an oasis in the sky.

Chapter 3

ABOVE: A contemplative garden benefits from a well-placed accent. Here, a sundial rests atop a pedestal overgrown with the crimson blossoms of a large-flowered clematis.

ABOVE RIGHT: Layers of deep green leaves punctuated by white blooms recall the shady silence of a forest glade. The stone path is cool underfoot, its gray slabs leading to an almost-hidden entrance.

Secret Spaces

COURTYARDS, WALLED GARDENS, AND OTHER GARDEN OASES

There is something about a secret garden, something magical and mysterious that reminds me of a sunlit clearing in a primeval wood. When I first read *The Secret Garden* as a child I was fascinated that the girl in the story was able to create the garden without grown-ups. Now that I am "grown up" myself, the book appeals to me for different reasons. A quiet, green spot, shielded from noise and traffic and all the cares of modern life, sounds wonderful to me! I've often longed for a bench under an apple tree where I could curl up with a book and be lulled by the scent of roses and the sound of bees. Small gardens are made to order for such satisfying spaces.

If you are lucky enough to have a courtyard or a space enclosed by walls or fences, the groundwork for your secret garden has already been laid. Structure is an integral part of any garden, and it is absolutely essential in gardens of this type. Enclosures are a necessity, although they need not surround the garden: a patio that is hidden from sight by a trellis, fence, or stone wall becomes a private place; a gazebo or an arbor framed in greenery and flowers can also stand alone as a secret space.

NEEDFUL THINGS

A seat of some kind is ideal, and provides cool respite in a shady spot. Opt for a bench of weathered teak, an old-fashioned swing-glider, or even a hammock. Because secret gardens are ideal for contemplation, a focal point such as a pond, gazing globe, sundial, or birdbath is also a nice touch.

TOP: Planting a flowering climber, such as this jasmine, on the adobe wall prevents this seating area from becoming too warm, as the foliage tempers reflected light from the solid wall. BOTTOM: Four ginkgo trees, twined with climbing roses and placed at the corners of a gravel square, create a shady private bower within an open-plan garden.

Establish a secret space by constructing a tall fence or hedge around your garden; then build an arch and plant it with vines that will grow into a thick tangle. The splash of color glimpsed through the narrow passage lures visitors to peek into a garden whose very inaccessibility makes it desirable. This sort of garden will provide luxurious refuge for those lucky enough to be invited inside.

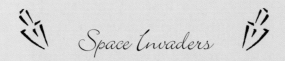

Lily-of-the-valley is sweetly scented but can spread out of control.

The one thing you don't want when gardening space is at a premium is a plant that is going to take over the place. Garden catalogs often don't tell you about them—the most you can do is watch for key words like "vigorous" and "spreading." Some invasive plants are beautiful and may still be worth planting—preferably in a container or in a planting area surrounded by concrete. Invasive plants may even be a plus: instead of purchasing the three to five perennials usually needed to create a visual effect, one will be more than enough! But some plants are so invasive that states have banned their sale; invasive exotics are squeez-ing out native plants all across the continent. A few troublemakers are listed here, but beware, there are a lot more waiting for an unsuspecting gardener to give them a little piece of land. Remember the old movie *Day of the Triffids*? How about *Land of the Loosestrife, Invasion of the Japanese Honeysuckle, Raspberry Reign of Terror, Horseradish Horror,* or *The Attack of the Beastly Bamboo*? Here are a few others to plant with caution:

BISHOP'S WEED (*Aegopodium podagraria*) I can't believe that this aggressive plant is actually sold in some catalogs. It does look nice in pictures, but when it is sunburned and wilted and strangling every other plant in the garden, believe me, it doesn't look nearly as nice.

BUGLEWEED (*Ajuga* spp.) This is an attractive groundcover but be selective in what species you choose to plant. The species *A. reptans* grows like a weed and is almost impossible to control when planted near a lawn; this includes the popular cultivars 'Bronze Beauty', 'Burgundy Glow', 'Multicolor', and 'Silver Beauty'. Unless you want a ground-cover that will spread over a large area, plant cultivars of *A. genevensis* (such as var. *rosea*) or *A. pyramidalis* ('Metallica Crispa').

COMFREY (*Symphytum* spp.) The herb known as boneset for its reputed medicinal qualities has been found in gardens since ancient times—once established, the ancient gardeners couldn't get rid of it! One reference book notes, "rhizomes give rise to unbranched stems resulting in rapidly spreading colonies." To say the least.

GOOSENECK LOOSESTRIFE (*Lysimachia clethroides*) Like obedient plant, this is very pretty and you should never need to plant more than one. If you have a spot (a big spot) where you never plan to plant anything else, you may want to try this. Unlike lily-of-the-valley, this plant may be controllable in the North but it's unstoppable further south.

JERUSALEM ARTICHOKE (*Helianthus tuberosus*) Here's a clue—when the catalog description says "needs considerable room," they aren't just referring to air space for the height of the plants. "Easy to grow" in this case means "just try and kill it."

LILY-OF-THE-VALLEY (*Convallaria majalis*) On the plus side, it smells wonderful. On the minus side, it is poisonous. Apparently this plant is not as invasive when grown in the South as it is in the North. If it is already planted when you move in, learn to love it.

LYTHRUM AND LOOSESTRIFE (*Lythrum* spp.) These pretty purple plants are becoming the kudzu of the Midwest. Some cultivars are suppos-edly sterile—don't believe it. It's illegal to plant these in some states.

MINT (*Mentha* spp.) There may be some mints that aren't invasive, but if that's the case I haven't found one yet. Plant this herb in a container to keep it from taking over your garden—some people plant containers of mint in the ground, but since mint is a root spreader I'd rather not take the chance on it taking root in the soil. Mint smells wonderful but attracts lots of bees, so don't put it where the bees will be a nuisance.

Be sure to plant some shrubs that will provide berries for birds and other wildlife, and flowers that will attract hummingbirds and butterflies. Strawberries, viburnums, and hollies, as well as countless other plants, are rife with berries that birds enjoy. Hummingbirds are drawn like magnets to trumpet-shaped flowers like gladioli, penstemons, and petunias. They're also partial to bright colors like the vibrant pink of fuchsias and mandevillas. Butterflies are sure to visit if you plant sweeps of bright-colored flowers, especially if you include a butterfly bush. They also like herbs such as lavender, and nectar-rich plants like honeysuckle.

LIVING WALLS

If you don't already have a fence or wall and don't want to add one (or if you live in an area where these structures are not allowed), you may choose instead to create a living enclosure with plants. Both hedges and faster-growing "walls" of vines are good choices for creating a sense of privacy.

Hedges can be trained to the height of your choice, although if you prefer a tall hedge it will probably take a few years to establish. For a traditional tall hedge, Hicks yew (*Taxus* × *media* 'Hicksii') is a good choice. This fast-growing conifer is narrowly columnar, and grows two to three times taller than wide. For a lower hedge, consider Brown's yew (*Taxus* × *media* 'Brownii'), a dense, slow-growing form that is almost globe-shaped. Gardeners in the South may have better luck with Japanese

plum yew (*Cephalotaxus harringtonia*), Chinese yew (*Taxus celebica* [syn. *T. chinensis*]), or smooth bark cypress (*Cupressus glabra*). Japanese cedar (*Cryptomeria japonica*) is also a recommended screening plant for southern zones, particularly the cultivars 'Benjamin Franklin', and 'Sekkan Sugi'.

For fast screening, American arborvitae (*Thuja occidentalis*) is an old favorite: 'Hetz's Wintergreen' is a very fast-growing, narrow, conical form; 'Sunkist' is another fast grower, and has golden yellow foliage; 'Techny' and 'Smaragd' are compact, conical forms. Western red cedar (*Thuja plicata*) cultivars

RIGHT: In this tiny walled garden a miniature gazebo draws the gaze down the path, visually lengthening the space. If you are including features such as gazebos, fountains, or statues, make sure that they are appropriate to the scale of the garden. An accent that is too large for its space will seem ungainly, and will only make the garden appear smaller.

such as 'Canadian Gold' and 'Hogan' are suitable for screening; so are Chinese junipers (*Juniperus chinensis*) such as 'Fairview', 'Pyramidalis', and 'Spartan', as well as the Eastern red cedar (*Juniperus virginiana*) cultivars 'Boskoop Purple' and 'Robusta Green'. An evergreen frequently sold for hedging is Lawson's cypress (*Chamaecyparis lawsoniana*); It has a weak root system, however, and is difficult to grow in many regions. Leyland cypress (*Cupressocyparis leylandii*) is a popular plant for fast screening but it is susceptible to winter damage.

As an alternative to a conifer hedge, broadleaf plants such as boxwood, holly, rhododendrons, or Japanese laurel (*Aucuba japonica*) work well in regions with mild winters. Deciduous shrubs suitable for hedges include Amur maple (*Acer ginnala*), winterberry (*Ilex verticillata*), American cranberry bush viburnum (*Viburnum trilobum*), Persian lilac (*Syringa × persica*), barberry (*Berberis* spp.), privet (*Ligustrum* spp.), cornelian cherry dogwood (*Cornus mas*), alpine currant (*Ribes alpinum*), and red chokeberry (*Aronia arbutifolia*).

Several viburnums work well as hedges or screens; since many alternatives are available, you can select a species that will do well in your region: choices include arrowwood viburnum (*V. dentatum*); a hybrid

Flowering shrubs make especially lovely screens, contributing seasonal color as they shield the garden from view and reduce noise from traffic and passersby. These azaleas and rhododendrons in shades of yellow, magenta, and peach provide a dense cover throughout the flowering season.

of the wayfaring tree (*V. lantana* 'Mohican'); European cranberry bush (*V. opulus*); and Allegheny viburnum (*V. rhytidophylloides*). Viburnums grown for their flowers and fragrance include *V. burkwoodii* 'Mohawk', *V. carlesii*, and *V. juddii*.

For an old-fashioned flowering hedge, consider bridal-wreath spirea (*Spirea prunifolia*) or a hedge of roses—'F.J. Grootendorst', 'Thérèse Bugnet', and 'The Fairy' are just a few possibilities.

Add ambience to your secret garden by planting several vines: clematis will twine through bushes as well as up trellises, honeysuckle works well in partly shaded gardens, and Boston ivy will quickly cover a brick wall. English ivy (*Hedera helix*) may not survive a cold winter, while trumpet vine and silver lace vine might take over the place. Vines such as kiwi and climbing hydrangea are slow to establish but worth it when they finally take off. Climbing roses and wisteria look great, but be careful—they are extremely heavy and many readymade arbors and trellises could collapse under their weight.

ADDING A BERM
Another simple way to create a secret space where walls are not practical is by installing a berm, which is basically a raised bed without sides, although berms are sometimes outlined in brick or stone. Berms add interest to flat gardens by changing the grade, and in yards with heavy clay soil, compacted soil, or poor drainage, a berm can mean the difference between plants living and dying.

Because of the weight of the soil, berms are usually not an option for balcony or rooftop gardens, but even the tiniest city or suburban garden can benefit from a berm, especially since this versatile feature can be constructed in whatever shape, size, angle, and location you select. Berms are usually between 4 and 8 inches (10 and 20cm) above the ground at their highest point; the soil will warm up quickly in the spring but because of the sharper drainage angle it will also dry out quickly. Berms and raised beds also make gardening accessible to those who find bending painful. Since soil is added to create the berm, you can easily amend the soil from the start to suit the specific needs of the plants you plan to use—this is much simpler than double digging in clay soil.

In neighborhoods where fences aren't allowed, consider planting a sunny berm with tall ornamental grasses such as *Miscanthus* or tall-growing perennials such as Joe-Pye weed (*Eupatorium purpureum*), queen-of-the-prairie (*Filipendula rubra*), or colewort (*Crambe cordifolia*) to create a wall of plants. For a real conversation piece, try planting *Gunnera manicata*, a fairly tender plant (Zones 7 to 10) that grows up to 8 feet (2.4m) tall and has individual leaves that measure as much as 6 feet (1.8m) across.

SELECTING A THEME

Secret spaces are the perfect places to plant theme gardens, indulging all your garden fantasies without worrying that you're carrying the theme too far. Working within a well-defined space, it becomes relatively easy to create a moonlight garden of white

and night-blooming flowers; a minimalist Japanese garden with raked stones and a few perfect plants; a garden of dwarf conifers, heaths, and heathers; an herb garden; a cutting garden; or a garden of everlastings.

A theme also provides you with instant direction and cohesion for your garden design. Rather than seeking out all the plants that would grow in your sunny courtyard, focus on those that match your chosen theme, be it a hot color planting or a Shakespeare garden.

FUNCTIONAL FEATURES

Floodlights or Japanese lanterns placed among trees can add drama to a nighttime garden, while ground-level solar lights can outline a path or pond. Make sure the shape and style of your secret space are compatible with the architecture of the building and blend with the rest of the garden.

Garden structures should not just be stuck in as a centerpiece; they should be functional, if possible. If you like to entertain, make sure your gazebo is large enough to seat a few friends; if you have a hot tub or pool, wrap the garden around it.

If children will be using the garden, consider building a tree house or freestanding playhouse within an enclosed space. Don't exclude children from your gardening endeavors. There are several excellent books that offer great suggestions for involving kids in planting; creative ideas range from constructing a twig teepee and training fast-growing vines up the sides to planting a "house" of tall sunflowers twined with morning glories.

A secret garden should be a private place for dreaming or sitting with friends, a place for contemplation and meditation cut off from the workaday world. Within the framework of hedges or walls, trellises and vines, a gardener can paint with foliage and flowers to create his or her own image of Eden.

ABOVE: Astilbes and ferns shelter a small garden light. If you plan to spend evening time in your garden, lights make excellent additions to the landscape. Choosing a decorative garden light will allow it to serve as an accent during the day and a functional feature at night. OPPOSITE: A low stone wall encloses this springtime garden of hostas, tulips, and pansies sprawled under a flowering dogwood tree. A raised bed—or a berm, if you prefer not to construct sides for your bed—can serve to separate your garden space from the yard next door without creating the impression of a barrier. If you prefer a bit more privacy for your yard, the bed or berm can be planted with ornamental grasses or other tall plants that will make effective screens.

Chapter 4

ABOVE: Ornamental grasses are used to stunning effect on this wooden deck. The varying textures, colors, and forms of the grasses are accentuated by placing them at different heights, a tactic that creates "movement" in the arrangement and makes it more interesting visually.
ABOVE RIGHT: Large-flowered purple clematis clamber up a trellis, welcoming visitors to this southwestern-style home while providing a touch of privacy to the porch.

Gardens for Outdoor Rooms

LANDSCAPING FOR PATIOS, DECKS, AND PORCH SURROUNDS

Relaxing with a morning cup of coffee or an afternoon glass of iced tea out on the porch is one of the premier pleasures of summer, and how much more enjoyable it is when your porch, deck, or patio is surrounded by plants that beautify the view and perfume the air. There are a few basics that can help you enhance the environment surrounding your "outdoor room," thereby creating a more pleasant retreat.

Flowers and foliage can improve the look of your porch or patio. Your plantings may complement an architectural feature of your house or hide a multitude of flaws. Or

use plants to screen the empty space below your porch or deck. Creative plantings can also soften the severe lines of a structure.

Years ago, foundation plantings of juniper and yew were designed to cover ugly, exposed foundations that are not as commonly seen in today's residential structures. While setting too many plants too close together and too close to the house is still a common landscaping problem, most houses would look bare without some kind of planting nearby. If you have a small ranch house, though, consider how it will be dwarfed if you plant a white pine near

Vines and climbers are valuable plants for any area of the garden, but are especially useful in the areas surrounding porches, decks, and patios. These versatile plants add a lovely vertical dimension to the garden, and can be found in an astonishing variety of flower colors and forms. There are some, such as trumpet vine and Japanese honeysuckle, that are rampant growers and will take over the space, but others behave with much more decorum. Following are some climbers that are suitable for a small garden.

AMERICAN BITTERSWEET (*Celastrus scandens*) Insignificant, cream-colored flowers; autumn fruits in red and orange; dark green leaves

ARMAND CLEMATIS (*Clematis armandii*) White or pink-tinged flowers; dark green, evergreen leaves

BIG-PETALED CLEMATIS (*Clematis macropetala*) Pink or blue flowers; attractive, fluffy seedheads; light green leaves

BOSTON IVY (*Parthenocissus tricuspidata*) A hardy, fast-growing vine that turns brilliant shades of red in the fall; small three-pointed leaves

CAROLINA JESSAMINE (*Gelsemium sempervirens*) Yellow, tubular flowers; evergreen foliage

CLIMBING HYDRANGEA (*Hydrangea anomala petiolaris*) White flowers; dark green, heart-shaped leaves

CUP-AND-SAUCER VINE (*Cobaea scandens*) Bell-shaped flowers that are yellow-green upon opening but darken to purple; light green leaves

CYPRESS VINE (*Ipomoea quamoclit*) Small bright red flowers; threadlike green foliage

ENGLISH IVY (*Hedera helix*) Insignificant greenish yellow flowers; evergreen leaves

GOLDFLAME HONEYSUCKLE (*Lonicera × heckrottii*) Trumpet-shaped flowers; buds are deep red but open to creamy blossoms; attractive blue-green leaves

HYACINTH BEAN (*Dolichos lablab*) Light purple flowers; purple pods; dark green leaves veined with purple

ITALIAN CLEMATIS (*Clematis viticella*) Small purple flowers; medium green leaves

MOONFLOWER (*Ipomoea alba*) Large, white, night-blooming flowers; light green leaves

MORNING GLORY (*Ipomoea tricolor*) White, pink, or blue flowers; heart-shaped green leaves

ORNAMENTAL GRAPE (*Vitis coignetiae*) Insignificant flowers; deep blue, inedible fruits; dark green leaves that turn red in autumn

SCARLET RUNNER BEAN (*Phaseolus coccineus*) Scarlet flowers; green pods; medium green leaves

SWEET AUTUMN CLEMATIS (*Clematis maximowicziana*) Small white flowers; dark green leaves; fast grower

TALL NASTURTIUM (*Tropaeolum majus*) Red, orange, yellow, or creamy flowers; round green leaves

Honeysuckle sprawls effusively over an iron fence, the warmth of its blossoms intense against white brick.

The perfectly formed petals of 'Climbing Ole' are enough to inspire anyone to plant a rose or two.

it—a tree that could someday reach 100 feet (30m) tall. Trees, shrubs, and perennials planted near the house should be used to create welcoming entranceways, to keep the *house in balance with the plantings, and to* create an effect that will enhance the whole setting by creating a bond between the house and the landscape that surrounds it. The yard and garden should work together, forming an extension of the living area that is equivalent to an outside room, blending with the overall design of the house and adding to its ambience.

SCREENING

If you plan to spend a lot of time gazing at your garden from your porch or deck, remember that shrubs or trees that grow tall will limit views. You won't want your plantings to grow much above the floor level of your porch for the best views.

You may, on the other hand, wish to screen your porch with plantings, allowing this outdoor space to become a private place. Latticework between the railing and ceiling will provide a place for vines and climbers to creep, and is decorative in its own right. If you choose a slower-growing climber such as clematis or climbing hydrangea (*Hydrangea petiolaris*), you might want to twine through a fast-growing annual vine as well, for quick coverage. Try morning

(*continued on page 63*)

You can almost hear the rocking chairs creaking behind the lush green foliage and brilliant summer colors of this porch planting.

Plants That Make Scents

If fragrance meant the same thing to everyone, there would be only one perfume at the cosmetic counter. The sense of smell is personal and very evocative, able to bring back memories with uncanny accuracy. Sensitivity to scent varies dramatically from person to person—some claim to have no sense of smell at all, while others are able to detect the faintest of perfumes. Fragrance can be a powerful element in a garden, especially if scented plants are installed where the prevailing wind will carry the perfumed air near a porch, window, or deck. Some plants release their fragrance when the foliage is brushed, handled, or stepped on; these should be placed where people will pass close by. Nighttime can be magic in the garden—pale flowers reflect moonlight, and many release their strongest perfume after dusk. Before planting fragrant flowers or foliage plants, make sure that its scent is not objectionable to you—a perfume that is perceived as wonderfully fragrant by one person may be as pungent as skunk cabbage to another.

The following plants are well known for their contributions to the fragrant garden.

HERBS

Anise (*Pimpinella anisum*)
Caraway thyme (*Thymus herba-barona*)
Catnip (*Nepeta cataria*)
Chives (*Allium schoenoprasum*)
Clary sage (*Salvia sclarea*)
Coriander (*Coriandrum sativum*)
Creeping thyme, mother of thyme (*Thymus serpyllum*)
Cumin (*Cuminum cyminum*)
Dark opal basil (*Ocimum basilicum* 'Purpureum')
Dill (*Anethum graveolens*)
Garden sage (*Salvia officinalis*)
Holy basil (*Ocimum sanctum*)
Hyssop (*Hyssopus officinalis*)
Inca marigold (*Tagetes minuta*)
Lavender (*Lavandula angustifolia*)
Lavender cotton (*Santolina chamaecyparissus*)
Lemon-scented thyme (*Thymus* × *citriodorus* 'Doone Valley')
Lemon verbena (*Aloysia triphylla*)
Marjoram (*Origanum majorana*)
Mints: apple, chocolate, lemon, penny royal, peppermint, and spearmint (*Mentha* spp.)
Oregano (*Origanum vulgare*)

Pineapple sage (*Salvia elegans*)
Rosemary (*Rosmarinus officinalis*)
Rue (*Ruta graveolens*)
Scented geraniums: apple, apricot, chocolate, cinnamon, citronella, lemon, lemon rose, nutmeg, orange, pine-scented fernleaf, strawberry, and velvet rose (*Pelargonium* spp.)
Sweet basil, also lettuce-leaf basil (*Ocimum basilicum* var. *crispum*)
Sweet or tarragon-scented marigold (*Tagetes lucida*)
Thyme (*Thymus* spp.)
Wild garlic (*Allium sativum*)
Winter savory (*Satureja montana*)
Wormwood (*Artemisia absinthium*)

ANNUALS, BIENNIALS, AND PERENNIALS

Anemone clematis (*Clematis montana*, also var. *rubens*)
Arabian jasmine (*Jasminum sambac*)
Bee balm (*Monarda didyma*)
Carnation, clove pink (*Dianthus caryophyllus*)
Cheddar pink (*Dianthus gratianopolitanus*)
Chinese peony, cultivars such as 'Festiva Maxima' (*Paeonia lactiflora*)

RIGHT: Shrubby 'Hidcote' lavender spills its fragrant flowers over a garden path. FAR RIGHT: Woodbine honeysuckle (Lonicera periclymenum 'Serotina') *can climb up to 20 feet (6m) and blooms abundantly into the autumn.*

Common hop vine (*Humulus lupulus*)

Common jasmine (*Jasminum officinale*)

English chamomile (*Chamaemelum nobile*)

English primrose (*Primula vulgaris*)

Flowering tobacco (*Nicotiana alata*)

Fragrant starflower (*Nicotiana sylvestris*)

Heliotrope (*Heliotropium arborescens*)

Hyacinths (*Hyacinthus* cultivars)

'Hyperion' daylily (*Hemerocallis* × 'Hyperion')

'Ice Carnival' daylily (*Hemerocallis* × 'Ice Carnival')

Lily-of-the-valley (*Convallaria majalis*)

Mignonette (*Reseda odorata*)

Night-scented stock (*Matthiola bicornis*)

Orange daylily (*Hemerocallis aurantiaca*)

Oriental clematis (*Clematis orientalis*)

Orris root (*Iris florentina*)

Passionflower vine (*Passiflora caerulea*)

Poet's narcissus (*Narcissus poeticus* cultivars)

Potato vine (*Solanum jasminoides*)

Royal lily (*Lilium regale*)

Solomon's seal (*Polygonatum odoratum*)

Sweet autumn clematis (*Clematis terniflora*)

Sweet violet (*Viola odorata*)

Sweet woodruff (*Galium odoratum*)

Tuberose (*Polianthes tuberosa*)

Water lily (*Nymphaea odorata*)

White dittany (*Dictamnus albus*)

ROSES

Cabbage rose (*Rosa centifolia*)

China rose (*R. chinensis*)

Damask rose (*R. damascena*)

Floribunda rose cultivars, including 'Gruss an Aachen', 'Intrigue', and 'Saratoga'

Grandiflora rose cultivars, including 'Queen Elizabeth' and 'White Lightnin'

Hybrid tea rose cultivars, including 'Blue Moon', 'Charlotte Armstrong', 'Chrysler Imperial', 'Dolly Parton', 'Double Delight', 'Fragrant Cloud', 'La France', 'Mr. Lincoln', 'Pink Peace', 'Sutter's Gold', 'Sweet Surrender' and 'Tiffany'

Japanese rose (*R. rugosa*)

Musk rose (*R. moschata*)

Provence rose (*R. gallica*)

SHRUBS AND TREES

Burkwood daphne (*Daphne* × *burkwoodii*)

Buttercup winterhazel (*Corylopsis pauciflora*)

Butterfly bush (*Buddleia davidii*)

Carolina allspice (*Calycanthus floridus*)

Fragrant wintersweet (*Chimonanthus praecox*)

Franklin tree (*Franklinia alatamaha*)

French lilac (*Syringa vulgaris*) cultivars, including 'Adelaide Dunbar', 'Charles Joly', 'Congo', 'Katherine Havemeyer', 'Ludwig Spaeth', 'Miss Ellen Willmott', 'President Grevy', 'President Lincoln', and 'Vestale'

Garland flower (*Daphne cneorum*)

Japanese snowbell (*Styrax japonicus*)

Japanese tree lilac (*Syringa reticulata*)

Judd viburnum (*Viburnum juddii*)

Koreanspice viburnum (*Viburnum carlesii*)

Littleleaf lilac (*Syringa microphylla*)

'Miss Kim' lilac (*Syringa patula* 'Miss Kim')

Persian lilac (*Syringa* × *persica*)

Sourwood (*Oxydendron arboreum*)

Southern magnolia (*Magnolia grandiflora*)

Southernwood (*Artemisia abrotanum*)

Spicebush (*Lindera benzoin*)

Star magnolia (*Magnolia stellata*)

Sweet olive (*Osmanthus fragrans*)

Sweet pepperbush (*Clethra alnifolia*)

Winter honeysuckle (*Lonicera fragrantissima*)

Woodbine honeysuckle (*Lonicera periclymenum*)

Thyme releases its scent when brushed against and is sturdy enough to survive some trampling—for extra fragrance plant low-growing thyme between the pavers of the path leading to your porch.

glory (*Ipornea* spp.), with its trumpet-shaped blooms in shades of blue, purple, pink, and white; scarlet runner bean (*Phaseolus coccineus*), which boasts bright orange to scarlet flowers and edible beans; or hyacinth bean (*Dolichos lab-lab*), with its flowers of lilac and white, purple-veined leaves, and deep purple beans.

Vines and climbers can also be planted to offer privacy around a patio space. Sturdy trellising gives ample support for most climbing plants; alternately, you might construct a decorative fence that can serve as a frame for vines to climb.

A SHADY SPOT

A sunny patio will benefit from a patch of shade, which you can create by adding a pergola and training vines to grow across its top. Pergolas can be either freestanding or attached to the roof of the house at one side, providing shelter for a bench or a table and chairs. This leafy bower will beckon on scorching days, luring you with the promise of a cooling respite from the summer sun.

COLOR AND SCENT IN YOUR GARDEN

When planning plantings for your porch, deck, or patio, make sure to consider color and scent.

As interior decorators well know, color can greatly alter the mood of a room, and this is no less true of an outdoor room. Greens contribute a sense of serenity and restfulness, while reds, oranges, and yellows brighten a space. Let the style and color scheme of your house and any adjoining

ABOVE: Decks and their surroundings are ideal for small gardens—the wood makes a natural backdrop for plantings, while the flowers and foliage can be used to cover exposed areas at the base of the deck. OPPOSITE: This creative fence combines several ingenious features: latticing provides sturdy support for a variety of climbers, while a bracketed top shelf is home to a line of trough-shaped planters. Canary-bird vine clambers up the fence and is met by trailing scented geraniums, which overflow from the planters perched on high. If you are planning this type of construction, make sure that the fence is stable and the planters are secured.

spaces inform your decisions about the color of your planting scheme. Red and other bright colors look great against walls of white or earth tones such as adobe; pink and white blooms jump out when set against green or blue walls or when the plants are situated in a shady spot; and variegated or textured greens enhance almost any outdoor decor.

If the garden will be near a path, porch, patio, or any place where people will be passing by, include a few scented plants that will release their fragrance when brushed against. Creeping thyme, planted between flagstones or along a sidewalk, looks pretty in foliage and flower and is fragrant, too. The season of scent can be extended by planting hyacinths and narcissus to bloom in spring, followed by a late-blooming lilac. Roses such as the hybrid tea 'Mr. Lincoln' are heavily scented, as are many of the old roses such as the White Rose of York (*Rosa alba* 'Semi-Plena'). Roses need lots of water, fertilizer, and at least six hours of sunshine; they also get quite large and thorny so plant them with care.

Whatever type of planting you select for your outdoor room, a little thought and planning will ensure a truly enjoyable garden space.

Since the patio is where most families spend their outdoor time, it's worth putting extra effort into "decorating" the area. Vines twining through railings, hanging baskets and window boxes brimming with glorious flowers, and pots filled to overflow contribute enchanting scent, color, and texture to this exuberantly planted patio.

Chapter 5

Entrance Gardens

CHARMING PLANTINGS FOR MAILBOXES, DOORYARDS, AND ENTRIES

ABOVE: The motif of sun rays on the door of this southwestern home seems to be reflected in the sunny raiment of blanket flower (Gaillardia), *purple coneflower* (Echinacea purpurea), *and black-eyed Susans* (Rudbeckia fulgida). *A cheerful planting of flowers is an instant boost for the spirits—place them near the door where you can enjoy them every time you arrive home.*

OPPOSITE: A short, rounded container of spiky Puya chilensis *contrasts cleverly with the rounded flower clusters of a tall blue hydrangea in this small entrance garden. Using pots in your entryway allows you to plant and replant with the seasons. If the plant seems to be failing, you can move it quite easily to a healthier spot.*

BELOW LEFT: Form overwhelms function as the prolific blooms of clematis and 'Bantry Bay' roses almost obscure the rustic door. While the effect is charming, this overabundance of flowers is appropriate only for a little-used side door. You can achieve a more restrained rose arch with some hard pruning.
BELOW RIGHT: The rich, rosy color of this azalea is echoed in the deeper tones of a clematis clambering up the wall behind it. Crowned with a square planter of yellow blooms, the scene offers an exquisite tapestry of colors, textures, and flower forms.

W hat could be more pleasant than coming home to a profusion of colorful blooms climbing your mailbox or wreathing your doorway, their delicate scents wafting on the breeze? Planting your entrance is the perfect way to get maximum enjoyment for a minimum of effort. Nearly any type of entranceway can benefit from a tiny garden, whether it's a series of pots lining the steps, an abundance of annuals ringing the lamppost, or a cheerful array of flowers and foliage decorating the front gate.

STRUCTURE

The size and shape of your entrance may be determined by boundaries such as a driveway, front path, fence, or your neighbor's lot line. Check to see if there are any zoning *(continued on page 72)*

Make coming home a special pleasure by planting a lively little garden near your mailbox. Here, a series of containers filled with petunias, violas, and an assortment of foliage plants creates a corridor of color and texture below a line of brightly colored mailboxes.

Two Plans for Mailbox Gardens

Mailbox gardens are a phenomenon that seems to have evolved mainly in the second part of this century. As people began to move to the suburbs, and as the suburbs began to encroach further into rural areas, curbside mailboxes became a common sight. The trouble is that, however functional mailboxes may be, when they come in the form of a metal box on a stick they can be something of an eyesore. Many people use their mailboxes to make an artistic statement—stenciling a wooden post or installing an ornately curled iron stand, setting the mailbox on top of tree trunks, milk cans, wagon wheels, or just about anything at the regulation height. The boxes themselves come in everything from basic black or gray to miniature cottages or cleverly painted cats. Budding artists often paint or decoupage their mailboxes, while others dress the boxes in decorative fabric or laminated paper covers that can be changed with the seasons. Hanging baskets often adorn the posts; some mailbox posts are even used to fly a flag.

However beautifully a mailbox is displayed, it still sticks out like a sore thumb. A true mailbox garden provides a great opportunity for gardeners with limited experience, space, or funds to get their feet wet. The same way bathers at the ocean's edge test the water with their toes, creating a mailbox garden is a great way to try new ideas without committing a lot of time, money, or effort to a full-scale garden plot. The same principles apply to the spaces around lampposts, and you can adapt these ideas for other areas, such as the small patch of ground that borders your driveway or the narrow strip that runs in between a sidewalk and the street.

Note: Both plans involve planting climbing vines around a mailbox post. In order to train the vines, it will be necessary to attach invisible thread or a nylon trellis to the crosspiece of the mailbox post, fastening these to the soil with earth staples or something similar. Alternately, a length of chicken wire about 30 inches (75cm) high can be wrapped around the post and fastened with wire twists.

PLAN A

This cheap and cheerful mailbox plan focuses on annuals that can be sown directly in the ground or started from seed in peat pots, then planted into the soil as soon as all danger of frost is past. If you start your seeds indoors, thin the seedlings and harden them off (let them adapt gradually to their new, colder environment by placing them in a cold frame for a few days) before transplanting them outdoors. If you don't have a cold frame, set the seedlings outside for a few hours each day before planting them outdoors.

Train vines by pushing them through the trellis—it is not necessary to tie them. By midsummer the vines will have almost completely covered the mailbox and post. Morning glory seeds have a very hard casing—you can increase the chance of germination by soaking the seeds in water overnight before planting them.

PLANT LIST

1. Morning glories (*Ipomoea* spp.) in mixed colors, (plant 6–8 inches [15–20cm] from the post)
2. Hyacinth bean (*Dolichos lablab*), (plant 6–8 inches [15–20cm] from the post)

3. 'Globosa Mix' globe amaranth (*Gomphrena globosa* 'Globosa Mix')
4. 'Sonata' dwarf mixed cosmos (*Cosmos* 'Sonata')
5. Tree mallow (*Lavatera* spp.) in mixed colors (underplant this section with regal lily [*Lilium regale*])
6. 'Rose Queen' cleome (*Cleome* 'Rose Queen')
7. 'Victoria' annual sage (*Salvia farinacea* 'Victoria')
8. 'Purple Wave' petunias (*Petunia* 'Purple Wave')

PLAN B

This mailbox garden plan uses old-fashioned "perennials in 1-gallon" [3.8l] size or larger if possible).

PLANT LIST

1. *Clematis × jackmanii* 'Hagley Hybrid' (plant 6–8 inches [15–20cm] from footing)
2. 'Ruby Moon' hyacinth bean (*Dolichos lablab*) (a fast-growing annual to add color the first year)
3. 'Blue Charm' speedwell (*Veronica spicata* 'Blue Charm')
4. 'Pink Mist' pincushion flower (*Scabiosa columbaria* 'Pink Mist')
5. 'Moonstone' peonies (*Paeonia* 'Moonstone')
6. 'Pink Beauty' boltonia (*Boltonia asteroides* 'Pink Beauty')
7. Russian sage (*Perovskia atriplicifolia*)
8. 'Bath's Pink' cheddar pinks (*Dianthus gratianopolitanus* 'Bath's Pink')

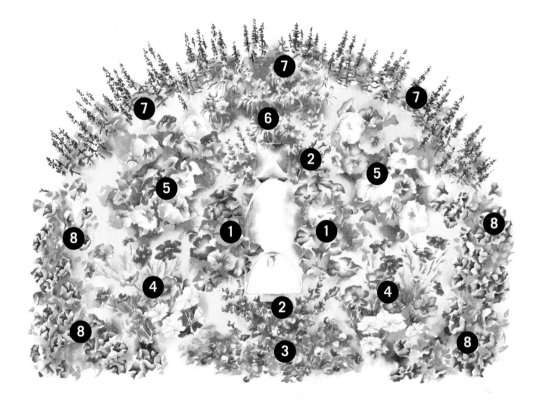

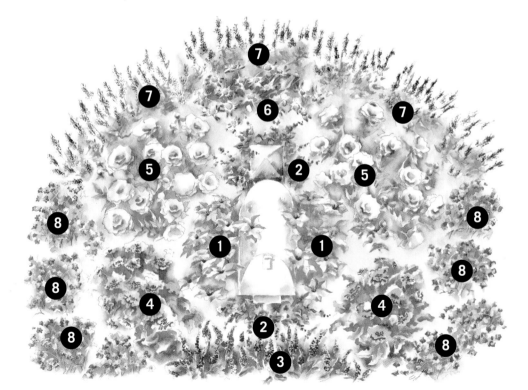

Dress the entry to your property with a sparkling array of seasonal hues. Like your interior decor, which is routinely supplemented with holiday ornaments, your entry garden can reflect the spirit of the season. Here, a potted collection of 'Golden Princess' spirea, **Dendranthemum** *'Esther', heath, and wintergreen brightens the passage through a farmhouse gate.*

restrictions that would apply to the size or form of your garden if you are planning to plant around the mailbox or along a right-of-way. When planting around the mailbox or a lamppost, note whether there are any drainage problems and whether there is excess concrete around the base of the post. If so, consider building up the soil into a small raised bed framed with bricks or timbers. Before you dig around a lamppost check where the wiring runs, so that you don't inadvertently hit a wire. As an extra safety measure, it's a good idea to cut electricity to the lamppost before you start. If you are planting around the mailbox, you'll probably have to supply extra supports for climbing plants. Attach a small trellis to the mailbox post, wrap the post with chicken wire, or use nylon trellis netting so vines can be trained to climb it.

PREPARATION

Mark off the outline of your proposed bed. Remove any grass or weeds from the area by digging them up. If you have time to kill, you can also rid the area of grass and weeds by laying black plastic over the spot, anchoring it with bricks or stones, and leaving it for a few weeks. Make sure to dig up the dead grass or weeds, in case only the surface layer was killed.

Serious gardeners use a method called "double digging" to prepare the soil. This adds valuable organic material and conditions the soil, so it's an excellent way to make sure your plants get the best growing conditions. It's not difficult to do, but it does require some time and effort.

After removing any grass or weeds from the area, dig down one spade's depth (about 12 inches [30cm]) and place the soil to the side of the bed on a tarp or sheet of heavy plastic. Once you've removed one spade's depth of soil, dig down a second spade's depth and place that soil on another tarp. Next, fork over the bottom of the bed with a garden fork, mixing in several inches of compost—anything from chicken feathers to worm castings to shredded leaves—as you go. Fill the bottom layer of the bed with the topsoil (the dirt that came from the top of the bed), continuing to mix compost in with the soil. Finally, replace the top level of soil with the subsoil, again mixing in plenty of compost. You now have a soil that is well conditioned and full of nutrients, a perfect growing medium for almost any plant.

If you are feeling lazy or have limited time, you can take a shortcut by adding compost or topsoil to build up a raised bed, or by mixing compost and good topsoil into a level bed.

MULCH

Lava rock, marble chips, gravel, pine needles, cocoa bean hulls, straw, shredded bark, black plastic, newspapers, and wood chips—all of these are forms of mulch. One of my favorite kinds of mulch is fallen leaves that have been mowed over until they are finely shredded. (Using leaves that aren't shredded blocks air and moisture, promoting disease.) Even grass clippings can be used, with caution—they may smell and they may contain weed seeds. If you mulch with grass clippings, wood, or a natural material in the

The Language of Flowers

Sweet peas sent a message of delicate pleasures to Victorian ladies well-versed in the language of flowers.

A dozen long-stemmed roses might be the way to "say it with flowers" today, but romantic souls in Victorian England developed a secret language meant to communicate every nuance of their emotions. Complex messages were communicated by flowers, either individually or in a bouquet. Many times a floral question was answered with a floral reply—the Victorians saw nothing wrong with a woman sending a floral tribute to a male admirer. These floral "codes" have been passed down over the generations and continue to strike a sentimental chord. It is easy to put together a private message by plucking a bouquet from an old-fashioned cottage garden—even trees and shrubs may have a tale to tell!

American linden . . . . Matrimony
Apple blossom . . . . Preference, I prefer
you before all
Arborvitae . . . . Unchanging
friendship

Azalea . . . . Temperance
Begonia . . . . Dark thoughts
Bellflower (white) . . . . . Gratitude
Boxwood . . . . Stoicism
Butterfly weed . . . . Let me go
Camellia (white) . . . . Unpretending
excellence
Candytuft . . . . Indifference
Canterbury bell . . . . Acknowledgment,
message received
Carnation (red) . . . . Alas, my poor
heart; my heart
aches for you
Chrysanthemum . . . . . . Slighted love;
(yellow) a heart left to
desolation
Chrysanthemum . . . . . . Truth
(white)
Clover (white) . . . . Think of me
Columbine . . . . Folly
Coreopsis . . . . Always cheerful
Daisy (white) . . . . Innocence
Dogwood . . . . Durability
Fern . . . . Sincerity
Flowering almond . . . . . Hope
Forget-me-not . . . . True love; do not
forget
Foxglove . . . . Insincerity
Fuchsia . . . . I like your taste
Globe amaranth . . . . Unchangeable,
immortality
Heath, heather . . . . Solitude
Heliotrope . . . . Devotion; I adore
you
Hibiscus . . . . Delicate beauty
Hydrangea . . . . Heartlessness
Iris . . . . A message for thee
Ivy . . . . Friendship, fidelity,
marriage

Lavender . . . . Distrust
Lilac (purple) . . . . First emotions of
love
Lily-of-the-valley . . . . . . Return of happiness
Meadowsweet . . . . Uselessness
Morning glory . . . . Affectation
Nasturtium . . . . Patriotism, splendor
Orange blossom . . . . . . Purity, bridal
festivities
Pansy . . . . Thoughts
Peach blossom . . . . I am your captive
Peony . . . . Shame, bashfulness,
ostentation
Periwinkle (blue) . . . . . . Early friendship,
sweet memories
Petunia . . . . Never despair
Phlox . . . . Our hearts are
united
Rose ('Boule de Neige') Only for thee
Rose (musk) . . . . Capricious beauty
Rose (red) . . . . Love
Rose (yellow) . . . . Jealousy, decrease of
love, infidelity
Rosebud (white) . . . . . . A heart ignorant
of love
Rudbeckia . . . . Justice
Salvia (red) . . . . Forever thine
Sweet alyssum . . . . Worth beyond
beauty
Sweet pea . . . . Delicate pleasures
and departure,
a meeting
Sweet violet . . . . Modesty
Veronica . . . . Fidelity
Weigela . . . . Accept a faithful
heart
Zinnia . . . . Thoughts of absent
friend

Old-Fashioned Flowers

There is an old saying, "Be careful what you wish for, your wish may come true." Gardeners of the past wished for roses that would flower all summer, for plants with predictable, perfectly shaped blossoms and clean foliage free from disease—plants that could resist drought or flood, heat or cold. As science brings us ever closer to the so-called "perfect plant," gardeners today are learning to appreciate plants of the past. Many old roses compressed all of their flowering into a week or two of riotous color, leaving the air heavy with fragrance. Not all old roses will survive sub-zero winters, even with protection—since roses don't usually cost much more than a flat of bedding plants, some cold-climate gardeners just treat them as annuals.

The garden flowers of old were often gloriously messy, spreading or self-seeding and popping up in unexpected places. Today perennials are expected to toe the line, staying put in neatly maintained beds and not outgrowing their welcome. Biennials are often brushed aside because their bloom can be less predictable than other plants, while interesting annuals lay forgotten in the midst of infinite impatiens and boring begonias. Some heirloom plants were introduced many years ago; others are natives that may have been here since time began. Seek out a few old-fashioned flowers, for old times' sake, and grow a bit of history in your garden.

FRAGRANT OR FLOWERING SHRUBS AND TREES

Amelanchier spp. (Serviceberry, shadblow, Juneberry)
Apple, 'Albemarle Pippin'
Apple, 'Esopus Spitzenburg'

The heady blooms of French hybrid lilacs such as 'Georges Bellair' inspire artists and gardeners with their springtime bounty.

Calycanthus floridus (Carolina allspice)
Cercis canadensis (Eastern redbud)
Cronus florida (Flowering dogwood)
Hydrangea arborescens 'Grandiflora'
Kalmia latifolia (Mountain laurel)
Malus × 'Bob White' (Crab apple)
Malus floribunda (Japanese flowering crabapple)
Philadelphus intectus 'Virginal' (Virginal mock orange)
Rhododendron prunifolium (Plum-leaf azalea)
Rhus aromatica (Fragrant sumac)
Syringa vulgaris (French lilac) hybrids and cultivars: 'Georges Bellair', 'Edith Cavell', 'Charles Joly'
Viburnum cassinoides (Swamp haw, Appalachian tea)
Viburnum opulus (Guelder rose)

OLD ROSES

'Archduke Charles' China rose
'Belinda' hybrid musk
'Belle de Crécy' Gallica rose
'Duchesse de Brabant' Tea rose
'Hermosa' China-Bourbon cross
'Konigin von Danemarck' alba rose
'Louise Odier' Bourbon rose
'Madame Alfred Carrière' Noisette climber
'Madame Hardy' Damask rose
'Madame Isaac Pereire' Bourbon rose
'Old Blush' China rose
'Old Pink Moss', sport of *R. centifolia*
'Reine des Violettes' hybrid perpetual rose
Rosa rubrifolia
'Zephirine Drouhin' Bourbon climber

OLD-FASHIONED ANNUALS, BIENNIALS, AND PERENNIALS

Alcea rosea (Single-flowering hollyhock)
Amaranthus caudatus (Love-lies-bleeding)
Aquilegia canadensis (Native columbine)
Callistephus chinensis (China aster)
Celosia cristata (Cockscomb)
Centaurea cyanis (Bachelor's button)
Consolida orientalis (Larkspur)
Dianthus barbatus (Sweet William)
Digitalis purpurea 'Alba' (White foxglove)
Dolichos lablab (Hyacinth bean vine)
Gomphrena globosa (Globe amaranth)
Heliotropium arborescens (Heliotrope)
Ipomoea purpurea (Morning glory vine)
Lavendula angustifolio (English lavender)
Lychnis chalcedonica (Maltese cross)
Lychnis coronaria (Rose campion)
Mirabilis jalapa (Four o'clock)
Nicotiana alata (Flowering tobacco)
Nicotiana sylvestris (Fragrant starflower)
Nigella damascena (Love-in-a-mist)
Nigella sativa (Nutmeg plant)
Phaseolus coccineus (Scarlet runner bean vine)
Sanvitalia procumbens (Creeping zinnia)
Scabiosa atropurpurea (Pincushion flower)
Tropaeolum majus (Nasturtium)
Zinnia pauciflora (Small-flowered zinnia)

process of decomposing, you will probably need to supplement the nitrogen in the soil. Gravel, marble chips, and lava rocks are best suited for areas without plants because they are high maintenance and won't inhibit weeds completely. These should be installed over a layer of black plastic for this reason.

Mulch can be added to your plant bed either before or after planting but be careful not to pile it up against the base of the plants. The benefit of adding mulch before planting is that you can just pile it on and smooth it out. The drawback is that you will have to scoop it out of the way as each plant is installed, and when you smooth it back afterwards it will be messy and mixed with soil. The drawback of applying mulch after planting is that you have to install it painstakingly by the handful around each plant. It's better to mulch later if you are sowing seeds directly into the soil, since seeds will not germinate under a layer of mulch. Also, if you are planting during a dry spell, water well before adding mulch so the maximum moisture will be held in the soil.

DESIGN

Working with plants is very personal— gardeners' favorites are often the old-fashioned plants they remember from childhood or those with evocative fragrances. The "best" color combinations and fragrances are often in the eye of the beholder. For example, I am not fond of spiky red salvias lined up like soldiers behind rows of neat orange marigolds; I prefer tall, yellow marigolds and annual blue salvias (not necessarily together). On the other hand,

I love the tangy smell of marigolds while many of my friends find it repellent. I find the kaleidoscopic colors of zinnias exhilarating while others find them garish. And while the best-selling, award-winning compact daylily 'Stella d' Oro' is the favorite of millions, I prefer the softer yellow of 'Happy Returns.'

If your garden pleases others, fine, but primarily it should please you. If you try a plant combination that doesn't work, move the plants around and try another one. I once read an interview with a longtime gardener who said he pictured his plants on roller skates and moved them whenever he felt like trying out a new design. Some plants, like peonies and the perennial gas plant, aren't fond of being moved, but most will adapt to their new homes nicely if the setting is right.

SELECTING PLANTS

Take a few minutes to find out your climatic zone (see page 114 to learn the plant hardiness zone for your region), soil type, and soil pH before making plant selections, also taking into consideration the amount of sun beating down on your chosen garden site. Bear in mind that certain plants are better adapted to nutrient-rich, acidic soil and shady sites, while others prefer full sun and average, alkaline soil, or something in-between. Annuals such as ivy geraniums, begonias, and impatiens may survive in full sun but will benefit from partial shade; likewise, hostas may live in full sun but will look much more lush and healthy when planted in the shade.

Tall purple irises lift their stately heads above a white picket fence. Sometimes the best designs are the simplest, and require nothing more than a mass planting of a favorite flower.

Which do you have in more abundance: time or money? If you have plenty of time and patience but little cash, try planting your garden with seeds. Seeds can be started simply in peat pots to be transplanted into the soil later, pot and all, or sown directly into the soil once the danger of frost is past. Planting from seed will reap the quickest results with annuals; perennials may take a year or more to flower. If you want the garden to come back by itself, either select reseeding annuals or plant perennials. Perennials are commonly sold in either 1-quart (9.5dl) or 1-gallon (3.8l) containers. The former cost less but may not flower the first year; the latter will cost more but should bloom right away. Spreading perennials may cost less to plant because you only need to buy one or two, but may cost more if you later try to eradicate them. Try using a combination of annuals and perennials; add a climbing vine for height and underplant with bulbs to extend the season.

Designing a mini-plot of your favorite plants to adorn the entrance to your house or yard guarantees maximum pleasure for a minimum of effort.

Chapter 6

ABOVE: The ornamental hot pepper 'Christmas' adds more than one kind of spice to a kitchen garden.
OPPOSITE: Terra-cotta pots make themselves right at home in herb gardens—these versatile containers here rest on a stone seat, within easy reach for harvesting.

Tiny Herb & Vegetable Gardens

GROWING EDIBLES IN PETITE PLOTS

Years ago, vegetable gardens were sprawling plots that could easily take up an eighth of an acre (506 sq m) or considerably more. In today's world of patchwork suburban lots, tiny garden enclaves in the city, and sky-high gardens on rooftops and balconies, large vegetable plots just don't make sense unless you are going into business. Once you've tasted vegetables fresh off the vine, though, it's hard to go back to plastic produce at the supermarket. This is one instance where the growers recognized a need and were quick to fill it—"baby" vegetables, container-grown fruits, compact tomato plants, and dwarf forms of just about everything else are now available. As gardening began to corner a growing market share, seed producers also recognized that ornamental vegetables would stand a better chance of being planted in gardens where space was at a premium. Assuming they both tasted the same, would you choose a messy-looking vegetable or an attractive one? Working on the assumption that cute and colorful sells in fruits and vegetables as well as flowers, a steady flow of tasty but ornamental edibles has become available.

For small-space gardeners, these tiny vegetables and fruits are ideal, whether they are grown as a food crop or just for looks. A small raised bed can hold an amazing number of these little plants, while gardeners without room for a raised bed can simply plant them in containers. A growing number of gardeners are so impressed with the ornamental value of these "new" edibles, they are incorporating them right into their

ABOVE: This regimented display of chard, carrots, brussels sprouts, and white alyssum has been planted according to height and habit, with the tallest, leafiest plant at the back and the low-growing flowers in the front. Unlike the widely spaced rows of a more traditional vegetable garden, this planting offers ornamental possibilities like those found in flower beds; the close spacing means that the overall planting requires less room than the usual vegetable patch. LEFT: Some vegetables will even grow happily confined to a container. These 'Painted Lady' scarlet runner beans are ornamental as well as edible, and mix well with flowers and other vegetables in this minute potted garden. OPPOSITE: Edibles and ornamentals blend beautifully in this tiny mixed perennial and herb garden. The color scheme, which combines shades of purple with an array of greens, keeps the planting from appearing overly chaotic.

ABOVE: Lettuce, nasturtiums, salvia, and 'Neon' and 'Orange King' pot marigolds are all elegant plants that please gardeners who appreciate the decorative qualities of many edibles. Combining usefulness and aesthetics in one plot is an practical approach for those with extremely limited space. RIGHT: This dwarf pear has been trained against a wall as an espalier. This system of training saves space and provides the trees with excellent care, allowing maximum production of healthy fruit in a small garden. Branches are selected and trained flat against a support (in any number of shapes, either horizontal or vertical) by pinching back unwanted growth. The fruit is then allowed to form at measured intervals along the branches.

flower borders. Alpine strawberries, for example, can be used as edging plants: the small fruits of these fraises des bois are pretty when nestled in the leaves, but my son usually snaps them off for snacks as soon as they ripen if the birds don't beat him to it. Luckily the foliage is attractive all by itself. The fact that these baby fruits and veggies are tempting to kids who scorn the full-size versions is yet another plus. From 'Little Ball' beets to nugget-size 'Planet' carrots, there are miniatures in almost every type of vegetable.

FRUIT TREES AND SHRUBS

Fruit trees are also available in sizes suitable for small gardens or containers; the 'Colonnade'® apple tree produced by Stark Bro's grows only 8 feet (2.4m) tall by 2 feet (60cm) wide, yet if two varieties are planted for pollination the unlikely orchard will produce a satisfying crop of apples. Most dwarf trees aren't quite that narrow, but they should not grow much beyond 8–10 feet (2.4–3m) tall; these include dwarf apricots, nectarines, cherries, plums, and pears. Many new cultivars make it possible to grow these dwarfs in a much wider hardiness range than in the past; disease-resistant and self-pollinating cultivars are also available. For a special effect, not without work, consider espaliering fruit trees on a sunny courtyard wall, or training them to form arbors or gazebos. Fruit trees offer endless possibilities to small gardeners.

Blueberry bushes are so attractive they can be used as a hedge as well as in a kitchen garden; they have delicate creamy

flowers in spring and good autumn color. Think twice before planting blackberries or raspberries in a small garden, though—they can overrun the whole yard within a year or so, and while the fruit is wonderful, battling to keep the plants within their bounds is next to impossible. Grapevines and kiwi vines are often used to border gardens; although these may not take off the first year, the vines could soon become more than the small garden can handle without judicious pruning. Scarlet runner beans and hyacinth beans are prolific annuals; the beans, pods, and flowers are so attractive it's almost a shame to eat them. When planted on tall bean towers or teepees, they add an element of height to the garden.

There are flower gardeners and there are vegetable gardeners, and never the twain shall meet—at least, that's what many people used to think. Nowadays there are so many beautiful fruits and vegetables on the market, it's getting harder to tell which gardens are grown for food and which for looks. Gardeners with limited space can mix perennials, annuals, herbs, fruits, and vegetables into one all-encompassing plot. Instead of the mishmash they feared, these experimentalists find they have created a thing of beauty. Novice gardeners can start small with a vegetable plot, two dwarf fruit trees in containers (try apples, pears, peaches, or apricots), and a compact cutting garden. Add herbs like borage or nasturtiums for their edible flowers. To make the most of limited space, make sure to select plants with pizzazz—veggies can be beautiful, too!

BEAN, SCARLET RUNNER Thomas Jefferson grew this ornamental climber in his garden at Monticello and it's every bit as desirable today. Several cultivars are available—one is stringless, others have an early, heavy yield. A pollinator is needed for best results.

BLUEBERRIES Even if high bush blueberry bushes (*Vaccinium corymbosum* and others) did not provide fruit that is popular with both people and birds, they would still have a place in the garden. In spring they produce delicate creamy white to pale pink flowers and in summer a delicious fruit; in autumn the foliage turns a beautiful range of colors from pink and rose to orange and bronze. Browse through catalogs for a cultivar suited to your particular climate and soil conditions.

CAULIFLOWER, 'VIOLET QUEEN' HYBRID Toss some early-maturing purple cauliflower into a salad to really brighten it up, or cook it and watch it turn green.

EGGPLANT, 'MINI BAMBINO' HYBRID The dark purple fruits of this small plant are only an inch (2.5cm) across, making it a perfect choice for a patio container. With its large purple flowers and interesting fruits, this is a beautiful addition to the ornamental kitchen garden.

LETTUCE, 'SIMPSON ELITE' The frilled light green leaves of this lettuce make it as pretty as any edge-of-the-border perennial. This hybrid is an improved version of 'Black Seeded Simpson' lettuce, and has better heat tolerance.

PEA, ASPARAGUS The pods are ready to steam or stir-fry when they reach an inch (2.5cm) in length. With its deep red flowers, this plant makes an attractive groundcover.

PEPPER, HOT 'CHILTEPIN' This pepper makes a great container plant, with colorful fruits less than an inch (2.5cm) across. The chilies start out green, then turn from black to red. Hot stuff!

PEPPER, 'TEQUILA' HYBRID Wow! This pepper goes through a whole spectrum of colors, including green, light orange, red, and lavender before it matures to a luscious purple. The foliage is said to resist tobacco mosaic virus.

RADICCHIO, 'RED VERONA' Create an exotic salad with this striking plant. The heads turn burgundy in the autumn and are highly ornamental.

SPINACH, MALABAR 'RED STEM' This heat-loving plant will top 6 feet (1.8m) when trained against a fence or trellis. Its red stems are standouts against the dark green foliage, and it has a longer growing season than ordinary spinach.

SQUASH, 'SUNBURST' HYBRID What is green at both ends and yellow in the middle? These pretty, little, scalloped-edge butter-type squashes, that's what. Even though the fruits are small, squashes and gourds tend to be prolific climbers and spreaders.

SWISS CHARD, 'RHUBARB' As the name implies, the dark red stalks of this vegetable resemble rhubarb. The deep green leaves have red veins and add to the ornamental value of the plant. Both the stalks and leaves are edible and packed with vitamins. The cultivar 'Vulcan' is also recommended.

TOMATO, 'YELLOW CANARY' A tiny plant only 6 inches (15cm) tall, this miniature produces good quantities of bite-size yellow tomatoes. A real eye-opener!

Over the millennia, herbs have had a vast range of uses: they've provided seasonings to satisfy the taste buds, delightful aromas to soothe the soul, ornamental form and flowers to salve the spirit, and medicines to heal the body. Herbs have also been used as dyes and disinfectants; some have also served a less savory sideline as poisons and emetics. The vivid common names of many herbs provide clues to the purposes they served—from medicinal to magical—and legends about herbs abound. Here is a sampling of traditional uses for some herbs.

ABSINTHE The liqueur called absinthe was distilled from oil of the wormwood plant (*Artemisia absinthium*) and anise. In 1915 several countries, including the United States, banned the drink because it was found to result in wormwood poisoning. Imbibing too much results in complete paralysis or death.

BELLADONNA Also known as deadly nightshade, this plant (*Atropa belladonna*) was originally favored as a cosmetic eyedrop to enlarge the pupil and beautify the eye. A derivative of the plant is the drug atropin, which is both a heart stimulant and a poison.

GARLIC Potent and powerful, the garlic plant (*Allium sativum*) was believed to repel disease and dark forces, holding back everything from plague to vampires. Today, garlic is used to get rid of intestinal worms, relieve gas pains, and lower cholesterol levels in the blood.

GINSENG The name ginseng, originally *Jen-Shen*, or "Man-Root," is derived from a 2,500-year-old Chinese legend about a spirit that comes to earth in the human-shaped form of the ginseng root. Stories of ginseng's amazing powers aren't limited to China—in India the root was believed to ensure immortality. Cultivated ginseng is widely available but is reputed not to have the same qualities as wild ginseng (*Panax ginseng* and American ginseng, *P. quinquefolius*). Even today, licenses and restrictions apply to the collection of ginseng roots.

HEMLOCK The poison hemlock (*Conium maculatum*) that killed Socrates in ancient times was not the familiar evergreen, but a member of the carrot family that resembles Queen Anne's lace. Once used to prevent cholera and to cure hernias, epilepsy, and pleurisy, today conium is used as a powerful sedative.

MARJORAM Used as a flavoring, tea, and dye, marjoram (*Origanum vulgare*) was believed to ease toothache, to relieve colic and indigestion, and to heal bruises. In ancient times it was believed that if marjoram grew on a tomb, the entombed person was happy.

PARSLEY A common garnish today, parsley (*Petroselinum crispum*) was once used to heal snakebites, relieve stomachaches and coughs, treat head lice, and even as a freckle cream. In the darker past, parsley was associated with death, and transplanting it was considered unlucky, even deadly. Parsley tea is said to have soothing qualities.

PEONY A popular perennial today, the peony (*Paeonia officinalis*) was once considered a potent cure-all, able to ward off evil spirits and prevent epilepsy and apoplexy. In the Middle Ages it was common for people to plant peonies at night, believing that they would go blind if a woodpecker witnessed the planting.

RUE To rue has come to mean "to be sorry for," and for centuries the herb rue (*Ruta graveolens*) has been a symbol of repentance. Rue was considered a power for good, used to ward off evil and sprinkled with holy water in churches. Used as a disinfectant and a moth repellent, rue was also reputed to prevent nightmares and to be an antidote for venomous bites. Some people develop a rash from the herb and "rue the day" they handled it.

SAGE Considered one of the most powerful healing plants, sage (*Salvia officinalis*) was brewed as a common tea in ancient times to preserve health and increase longevity. Its botanical name originated from the Latin *salvare*, meaning "to save". Sage was used as a gargle to treat laryngitis and to whiten teeth, as a nerve tonic, as a protection against the plague, and as a cure for fever. Sage was also believed to improve memory and increase brainpower.

HERBS

Herbs have been traditional choices for small gardens for centuries; it's easy to copy a historical design, create your own knot garden, or execute the plan included here (see pages 88–89). If this formal approach is not for you, interplant your herbs among ornamentals or in containers. Many herbs have silvery or decorative foliage that perfectly complements their more boisterously flowered cousins. And don't discount the flowering talents of certain herbs—

(continued on page 86)

ABOVE: Herb gardens need not conform to a complex design—this circular brick path frames and contains the lush purple mounds of lavender. Benches are a welcome addition, giving hardworking gardeners a chance to relax, observe, and inhale the fruits of their labors. LEFT: Parsley is easy to grow in containers, and makes an attractive addition to the garden even without the wonderful bonus of its culinary value. By confining herbs to containers you can minimize the amount of space they take up in your kitchen garden.

Just because you've given your small garden over to the production of vegetables, don't ignore the possibilities for relaxation it can provide. This rustic twig bench set far inside a thicket of tomatoes is the perfect place to relax on a summer's day. The scent of warm, sun-ripened tomatoes and the hum of bees as they busy themselves about the garden are sure stress-relievers.

Grasses and ornamental herbs give this cottage garden an updated look that is both natural and fresh. Herbs are versatile plants that complement nearly any architectural or garden style.

chives, for instance, have beautiful purple, globe-shaped blooms, and pot marigolds (*Calendula officinalis*, often confused with the unrelated *Tagetes* species, also called marigolds) are well loved for their cheerful yellow faces. If you don't have space in the ground, herbs are just as happy in a sunny window box or in containers.

Most herbs do require at least five or six hours of sunlight, and they benefit from being pinched back. It is useful to keep herb gardens close to the kitchen, so that the cook can nip outside to gather seasonings or pluck a garnish. Bunches of herbs can be hung to dry from a balcony, a porch rail, or a kitchen drying rack, as well as from herb racks made expressly for drying plants.

A surprising number of herbs are hardy—tansy, for instance, is so vigorous that it will take over the garden if not restrained by a raised bed or container. Plants in the mint family can be equally invasive, so beware of these; to be on the safe side plant them in pots or in beds bordered by concrete. The flowers of mints are negligible but the foliage smells great.

COLORFUL VEGETABLES

Don't neglect the aspect of color in your kitchen garden. Ruby chard, pepper plants, and red ruffled 'Lolla Rossa' lettuce prove that vegetable gardens can be colorful even without the addition of annuals; other vegetables with colorful foliage include 'White Peacock' and 'Nagoya Red' kale. From eggplant to brussels sprouts, just about everything is available in assorted colors today. Tomatoes are now grown in

colors and sizes ranging from the traditional large red fruits to tiny gold "currants." Bronze fennel can be used to add height, while endive, chives, lavender, salvia, or ornamental kale makes a dramatic edging for the herb or vegetable garden.

No herb garden would be complete without several forms of basil—not only is it a popular herb for cooking, but it has a subtle aroma and is ornamental, too. Rosemary will grow in many parts of North America, but it is only hardy to Zone 8; in warmer regions it is often grown as a standard in containers.

From an ornamental standpoint, one benefit of planting a vegetable garden in a small space is that it will quickly be as lush and full as a mature garden. With good soil, adequate drainage, and lots of sunlight, most vegetables and herbs are also relatively easy to grow. Half the fun of creating a vegetable or herb garden is selecting the plants you like to cook with, to eat raw, or just smell. With the range of miniatures and ornamental fruits and vegetables to choose from, the planning is a gourmet's delight, and the garden becomes a wonderland for the senses.

This charming potager is a mass of greens and purples, accented by the bright golden blooms of California poppy. These plants—which include runner beans, cabbage, fennel, and kale—have leaves that are heart-shaped, blistered, feathery, or deeply veined, offering a tapestry of subtle foliage effects.

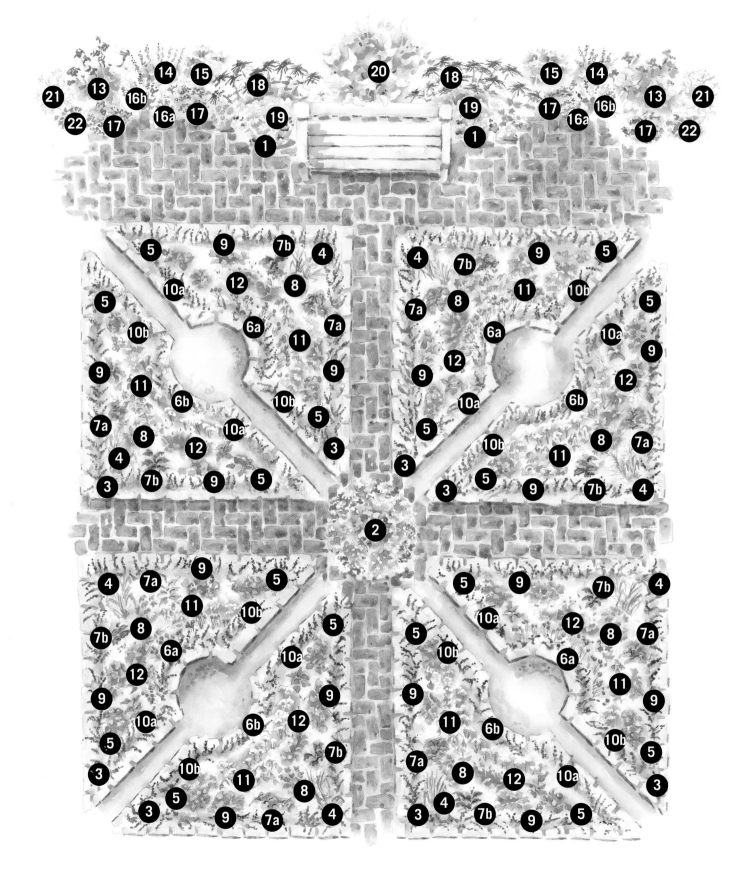

Herbal Knot Garden in Full Sun

A knot garden does not need to be difficult—you can copy a historical pattern or create your own. Define the edges with miniature hedges that thrive in your region—lavender, boxwood, santolina, rosemary, or germander are possibilities. Use wooden raised beds or paths of brick, gravel, stone, or mulch to define the garden's shape, depending on your budget and whichever material best suits the garden design. Clay brick is a classic, but if you have time, patience, and a touch of the artist in you, you can embed smooth rocks like cobblestones into the soil in an intricate design. The center structure can also vary—a gazing globe, sundial, sculpture, small tree, or large container can provide the central focus of the garden.

Most herbs do best in full sun and benefit from pinching back, something that will occur naturally if you use them for cooking. This garden incorporates edible herbs with others that are purely ornamental to create a garden that is pleasing to the senses. The knot garden is complete in itself, but if you have room, I have added an herb border with a bench so you can sit and admire your handiwork, surrounded by bees, butterflies, and wonderful scents. This garden will be at its best in the summertime.

PLANT LIST FOR CONTAINERS

1. Marguerites (*Argyranthemum frutescens*) grown as standards in pots and under planted with basket of gold (*Aurinia saxitalis*) and 'Cuty' horned violets (*Viola cornuta* 'Cuty').

2. Heliotrope (*Heliotropium arborescens*) grown as a standard in a large container, underplanted with marjoram (*Origanum vulgare*) and variegated oregano (*Origanum vulgare* 'Gold Tip'). Beside planter (either planted in the ground or set in wide, low containers) alternate plantings of 'Coccineus' lemon thyme (*Thymus serpyllum* 'Coccineus') and mouse-ear chickweed (*Cerastium bierbersteinii*).

   Also consider assorted mints (*Mentha* spp.) underplanted with 'Snowcloth Improved' alyssum (*Alyssum* 'Snowcloth Improved') and salad burnet (*Sanguisorba minor*).

PLANT LIST FOR THE KNOT GARDEN

3. 'Munstead' lavender (*Lavandula* 'Munstead')
4. French tarragon (*Artemisia dracunculus*)
5. 'Pink Panda' hybrid strawberry (*Fragaria* 'Pink Panda')
6a. Common chives (*Allium schoenoprasum*)
6b. Garlic chives (*Allium tuberosum*)
7a. 'Green Ruffles' basil (*Ocinum basilicum* 'Green Ruffles')

7b. 'Purple Ruffles' basil (*Ocinum basilicum* 'Purple Ruffles')
8. Rue (*Ruta graveolens*)
9. Assorted scented geraniums (*Pelargonium* spp.)
10a. Tricolor sage (*Salvia officinalis* 'Tricolor')
10b. German chamomile (*Matricaria recutita*)
11. Borage (*Borago officinalis*)
12. Lemon verbena (*Aloysia triphylla*)

PLANT LIST FOR THE HERB BORDER

13. Angelica (*Angelica gigas*)
14. Russian sage (*Perovskia atriplicifolia*)
15. 'Snowbank' boltonia (*Boltonia asteroides* 'Snowbank')
16a. Golden creeping thyme (*Thymus citriodorus* 'Aureus')
16b. 'Butterfly Delight Mix' hyssop (*Hyssopus officinalis*)
17. Thyme (*Thymus praecox*)
18. 'Violet Queen' bee balm (*Monarda didyma* 'Violet Queen')
19. Fernleaf dill (*Anethum graveolens*)
20. 'Ivory Silk' Japanese tree lilac (*Syringa reticulata* 'Ivory Silk')
21. Cilantro, also called coriander (*Coriandrum sativum*)
22. 'Powis Castle' artemisia (*Artemisia* × 'Powis Castle')

Chapter 7

ABOVE: Plants seem to grow up, over, and out of the stones themselves in this compact rock garden.
Even a small rock shelf will provide space for an alpine planting.
ABOVE RIGHT: The miniature blossoms of flowering plants pull rock garden visitors down
until they are eye-to-eye with these tiny treasures.

The Diminutive Rock Garden

ALLURING ALPINE PLANTINGS

There is a fascination with rock garden plants that collectors of porcelain miniatures or dollhouse fittings recognize easily. The minute petals seem impossibly tiny, flawless, and finely detailed. Maybe the plants seem so much more ethereal because their delicate flowers and foliage are often splayed against unyielding rock, or their blossoms are brilliantly outlined against gray stone walls. Mesmerized, we are pulled down onto our knees, using eyeglasses or magnifiers to get a closer look. When these tiny flowers are planted in the crannies of a rock wall or arranged to flow over the edge of a retaining wall, they come into our line of vision

ABOVE: Heaths and heathers make excellent rock garden plants for regions where soil and climate are suitable. Pictured here is 'Peter Sparkles' heather (Calluna vulgaris *'Peter Sparkles'). LEFT: Creeping conifers flow around rocks of different shapes and sizes, creating a river of green in this minimalist rock garden. OPPOSITE: In an arrangement reminiscent of a dry riverbed, this unusual sunken rock garden offers a multitude of interesting design possibilities. The stacked slabs of rock can be used as benches, while chunkier rocks overgrown with ivy supply contrast in form and color. Additional pattern and color are introduced with the red and black "hallway" of quarry tile that borders the miniature garden.*

Shallow containers make a home for sempervivums, pink **Aethinema pulchellum,** *and other rock garden plants in this pleasingly portable garden. Varying the sizes and heights of the containers creates a more dynamic setting and gives you freedom to choose plants of different sizes and habits.*

naturally. A rock garden is not the place for mass plantings of flowers, broad sweeps of foliage, or bold plant combinations. Not only are they all but impossible to execute in rocky outcroppings, but these brash displays look as awkward in a rock garden as Gulliver among the Lilliputians.

A ROCKY START

Small gardens and small plants are made for each other, pulling the line of vision into a tighter focus. The brilliant colors of tiny plants sparkle like jewels against the gritty gray backdrops of rocks and soil. If your small garden space is scattered with rocks, large and small, you have a lot going for you. You may even be lucky enough to have a stone wall with space between the stones, where you can create a special garden with a charm all its own.

If your rock garden site is sloped and has natural ledges and pockets filled with soil, all you need to do (and it's not as easy as it sounds) is evaluate the site to determine the plants best suited for it. If the ground is flat, consider bringing in a combi-nation of rocks and topsoil to change the grade in part of the garden. This allows you to plant tiers of flowers or plants spilling down a slope, giving the garden depth and a more interesting perspective. If topsoil needs to be added or existing soil needs to be amended, look for a gritty mix containing some sand or fine gravel to assure good drainage.

While in theory rock gardens should attempt to recreate the alpine or woodland conditions native to many diminutive plants, some succeed without a single plant of alpine origin—without even a rock. A rock garden without rocks? A wall of brick or stone might not have the same ambience as a rocky outcropping but just the same, an effective rock garden can be planted in the nooks and crannies and along the top of such a wall. Even a courtyard laid in brick can be turned into a rock garden, if there is room to squeeze tiny plants into the soil between the bricks. Fragrant creeping herbs like thyme are perfect for this type of planting.

Where drainage is a problem, rock gardens can be created by building up a berm of soil and supporting the sides with natural-looking rock. A type of rock called "holey boulder" is ideal for this, because hollows in the rocks can be filled with soil and planted with miniatures such as stonecrop (*Sedum* spp.).

Rocks of many shapes, sizes, and colors are available, but often it is both cheaper and easier to select rocks that originate nearby. It may be necessary to have heavy rocks installed by professionals, both to save your back and to ensure that the rocks are stable and set at the optimal angle to promote good drainage. Keep the layout as natural looking as possible by blending the rocks and soil artfully. As always, mulching will benefit the plants.

CONTAINER ROCK GARDENS

If you crave a rock garden but only have a rooftop, balcony, or concrete courtyard, use a trough or a series of containers. Bring the containers up to eye level, preferably at assorted heights, by placing them on pedestals, blocks of concrete, or other props. As with any container above the ground, be sure to have the weight distributed safely. A window box, a wide balcony ledge, or even a strawberry jar can hold a few small rock garden plants—there is really no garden too small to hold a rock garden, even though it might not be exactly traditional. If the only way you can have the garden you want in the space available is to break a few rules of design or tradition, so be it. The primary purpose of your garden should be to give you pleasure—if you like it and the plants are happy, that's what counts. In one sense a container rock garden is ideal, because you can customize the soil conditions the plants require; also, the

(continued on page 99)

Experimentation

The late garden writer Elizabeth Lawrence not only published books and newspaper columns, she carried on a personal correspondence with gardeners around the world and across the United States. Living in Zone 8, Lawrence was not in the ideal climate for a rock garden—her garden featured baking hot weather followed by periods of extreme humidity, not to mention heavy clay soil. Of her own somewhat lackadaisical soil preparation methods, Lawrence observed:

According to the British, who garden so sternly, the soil beneath the rock garden should be dug to two and a half feet and thoroughly mixed with compost. The rocks should be laid upon this with the special mixture for each type of plant in the spaces between. If I had waited to do all of this, I should never have had a rock garden. Mine was planted inch by inch, and I dug the stiff, rocky clay as deeply as I could (which in some cases, obviously, was not deep enough) and dug in sand and rotted leaves. Due to faithful mulching thereafter, the soil improved a little each year.

Lawrence found success with many little bulbs, and also noted that "there is an affinity between herbs and rocks." Although she reported problems growing *Aurinia saxatilis*, Lawrence found *Alyssoides sinuata* did well in her Raleigh, North Carolina, garden. She had raves for the South African annual *Diascia barberae* and called *Mazus reptans* "one of the best of the carpeters— I have never found fault with it."

Gardeners in all regions will experience frustration with some plants that are supposed to be easy, while successfully stumbling upon reportedly difficult plants that thrive. There is no formula for success with every plant in every region; you can read volumes about the plant but ultimately you won't know if it's going to work until you try it. For some reason rock gardening has a certain cachet—it is considered more artistic and more demanding than other types of gardening. For gardeners with small spaces, rock gardening has practical benefits; although you may have your head somewhere in the Alps, it helps to keep your feet firmly anchored on the ground.

Tiny Treasures

Picture a rocky slope in the thin, bright air of the Alps and you will be envisioning the quintessential rock garden. Alpine plants form the basis of most rock gardens and while these plants might be stuck at ground level, the gardens usually attempt to recreate the rocky, sunny conditions of a true alpine garden. Purists may draw back in dismay, but it is possible to create a rock garden even on the balcony of a high-rise apartment. The following list offers scores of plants that will look perfect in whatever type of rock garden you choose to plant.

ANNUALS AND PERENNIALS

Alpine barrenwort (*Epimedium alpinum* 'Rubrum')

Alpine forget-me-not (*Myosotis alpestris*)

Alpine pinks (*Dianthus* × *allwoodii*)

Alpine speedwell (*Veronica alpina* × 'Goodness Grows')

Auricula primrose (*Primula auricula*)

Baby's toes (*Frithia pulchra*)

Basket of gold (*Aurinia saxatalis*)

Blue corydalis (*Corydalis flexulosa* 'Blue Panda')

Candytuft (*Iberis sempervirens*)

Carpathian bellflower (*Campanula carpatica* 'Blue Clips', 'White Clips')

Cheddar pink (*Dianthus gratianopolitanus* 'Bath's Pink')

Coral bells (*Heuchera brizoides* × 'Chatterbox')

Cranesbill geraniums (*Geranium* spp.)

Creeping baby's breath (*Gypsophilia repens*)

Creeping phlox (*Phlox subulata*)

Creeping thyme (*Thymus serpyllum*)

Cushion spurge (*Euphorbia epithymoides* 'Polychroma')

Dalmatian bellflower (*Campanula portenschlagiana*)

Dead nettle (*Lamium maculatum* 'Pink Pewter')

Drumstick primrose (*Primula denticulata*)

English primrose (*Primula vulgaris*)

Geneva bugle weed (*Ajuga genevensis*)

Goldenstar (*Chrysogonum virginianum*)

Great Alpine rockfoil (*Saxifraga cotyledon*)

Hens-and-chicks (*Sempervivum tectorum*)

Hybrid daylilies (*Hemerocallis* spp. [Compact or dwarf hybrids])

Iceland poppy (*Papaver nudicaule*)

Irish moss (*Sagina subulata*)

Japanese spurge (*Pachysandra terminalis*)

Lamb's-ears (*Stachys byzantina*)

Lavender (*Lavandula angustifolia*)

Lewisia (*Lewisia cotyledon* 'Soranda')

Licorice plant (*Helichrysum petiolare*)

Lobelia (*Lobelia erinus* var. *compacta* 'Crystal Palace')

Moss campion (*Silene aucalis*)

Pasqueflower (*Pusillata vulgaris*)

Periwinkle (*Vinca minor*)

Pink candytuft (*Aethionema cordifolium*)

Polyantha primrose (*Primula* × *polyantha*)

Purple rock cress (*Aubretia deltoides*)

Pussytoes (*Antennaria dioica*)

Pyrenees thrift (*Armeria juniperifolia*)

Rock cress (*Arabis alpina*)

Rock rose (*Helianthemum* spp.)

Sea thrift (*Armeria maritima*)

Sedum (*Sedum reflexum*)

Serbian bellflower (*Campanula poscharskyana*)

Snow-in-summer (*Cerastium tomentosum*)

Spike speedwell (*Veronica spicata* × 'Waterperry')

Siberian squill (Scilla siberica)

Spiral bellflower (*Campanula cochlearifolia*)

Stonecrop (*Hylotelephium cauticolum*)

Sweet alyssum (*Lobularia maritima*)

Toadflax (*Linaria alpina*)

Woolly thyme (*Thymus pseudolanuginosus*)

Yellow corydalis (*Corydalis lutea*)

BULBS

Autumn crocus (*Colchicum autumnale*)

Caucasian squill (*Scilla mischtschenkoana*)

Crested iris (*Iris cristata*)

Crocus (*Crocus* spp.)

Danford iris (*Iris danfordiae*)

Glory-of-the-snow (*Chionodoxa luciliae*)

Greigii hybrid tulip (*Tulipa greigii* 'Plaisir')

'Hawera' daffodil (*Narcissus triandrus* 'Hawera')

'Minnow' daffodil (*Narcissus tazetta* 'Minnow')

'Pheasant's Eye' daffodil (*Narcissus poeticus* var. *recurvus* 'Pheasant's Eye')

Red star (*Rhodohypoxis baurii*)

Reticulated iris (*Iris reticulata*)

Siberian squill (*Scilla siberica*)

Snowdrops (*Galanthus nivalis*)

Snowflakes (*Leucojum vernum*)

Spanish bluebells (*Hyacinthoides hispanica*)

'Sundisc' daffodil (*Narcissus jonquilla* 'Sundisc')

'Tete a Tete' daffodil (*Narcissus cyclamineus* 'Tete a Tete')

Tuberous buttercups (*Eranthis cilicia*)

Waterlily tulip (*Tulipa kaufmanniana* 'Heart's Delight')

Wild onion or garlic chives (*Allium* spp.)

SHRUBS AND CONIFERS

Bosnian pine (*Pinus leucodermis* 'Schmidtii' [syn. 'Pygmy'])

Colorado spruce (*Picea pungens* 'Globosa')

Colorado white fir (*Abies concolor* 'Gable's Weeping')

Creeping broom (*Genista pilosa* 'Vancouver Gold')

Cryptomeria (*Cryptomeria japonica* 'Globosa Nana')

Eastern hemlock (*Tsuga canadensis* 'Gracilis')

English yew (*Taxus baccata* 'Amersfoort')

European larch (*Larix decidua* 'Corley')

Flaky juniper (*Juniperus squamata* 'Blue Star')

Flowering quince (*Chaenomeles speciosa*)

Heather (*Calluna vulgaris*)

Hinoki cypress (*Chamaecyparis obtusa* 'Nana Lutea')

Japanese red pine (*Pinus densiflora* 'Umbraculifera')

Japanese barberry (*Berberis thunbergii* 'Crimson Pygmy')

Japanese yew (*Taxus cuspidata* 'Aurescens')

Korean fir (*Abies koreana* 'Compact Dwarf' or 'Silberlocke')

Littleleaf boxwood (*Buxus microphylla*)

Norway spruce (*Picea abies* 'Gregoryana' or 'Procumbens')

Oriental spruce (*Picea orientalis* 'Aurea Compacta')

Rockspray cotoneaster (*Cotoneaster horizontalis*)

Savin juniper (*Juniperus sabina* 'Blue Forest')

Sawara cypress (*Chamaecyparis pisifera* 'Filifera Nana')

Slender deutzia (*Deutzia gracilis* 'Nikko')

Spring heath (*Erica carnea*)

White spruce (*Picea glauca* 'Rainbow's End')

Wintercreeper (*Euonymus fortunei* cultivars)

Snowdrops (Galanthus nivalis)

container can be moved around until it is in a spot that suits the plants and that is within your line of vision.

It is important not to overwater rock garden plants, so be sure the containers have drainage holes. Professional landscapers have mixed reviews about gravel set in the bottom of containers—some still feel that it helps the drainage, while others feel the drainage holes are sufficient and the gravel just takes away from root and soil space. Successful watering takes a light hand— don't allow the containers to dry out to the point that plants are wilting, since some may

not recover. When the soil is almost dry, slowly run water through the container until it is wet without being completely saturated. In hot weather it may be necessary to water once or even twice a day—with plants that little, there isn't much room for error.

SELECTING ROCK GARDEN PLANTS

Before you start to dig, either draw a plan showing roughly what you hope to create in your rock garden, or work it through beforehand in your mind if that's easier for you. Include plants for all seasons as well as

ABOVE: The other-worldly forms of sedums and houseleeks give this rock garden its startling aspect. Consider the colors, shapes, and textures of the plants you plan to include: a mixture of different forms that peak at different times throughout the seasons creates a garden with enduring interest. OPPOSITE: Eye-catching plants set among the rocks on this slope create a bit of Eden out of a difficult spot. Carefully chosen plants will hold the soil in place as well as beautify the hillside.

a variety of shapes and textures. Look for colors that will complement each other, whether they blend softly or light up the garden.

Prepare a list of plants that will survive in existing conditions, taking into consideration exposure, summer heat, winter cold, dampness, dryness, and other seasonal pleasures native to your site. This is the fun part—since you haven't actually purchased any of the plants yet, it's like a window-shopping expedition at the mall. Search through books, magazines, and plant catalogs until you get a fair idea of the types of plants you will need.

Be sure to shop from your list—it's all too easy to be suckered into buying a pretty little plant like creeping bellflower (*Campanula rapunculoides*) at the garden center, the one with the plant tag labeling it a 'spreader' and 'easy to grow.' Like many campanulas, creeping bellflower presents a pretty sight and is very hardy, too. Looks good, sounds good—so where's the problem? The flowers on the creeping bellflower might sell the plant to an unsuspecting customer, but the prepared shopper will know that this particular plant has rhizomes that spread like nobody's business and earn it the rating of a "weed." If it checks in to

your garden, it will never leave. A rock gardener who has done some homework would quickly discover that another fairly hardy plant, spiral bellflower (*Campanula cochleariifolia*), is extremely well suited for walls and rock gardens, as is the very hardy Serbian bellflower (*Campanula poscharskyana*). By reading up on plants at home, it is easy to select those that please you without being distracted from their true nature.

Since books and magazines are not usually in the business of selling plants, their descriptions tend to be less predictable (gardeners in different regions are bound to have different results), colors less vivid but more realistic, and problems less obscured by sales tactics. Once you've narrowed down the plants that are tiny enough for a

rock garden and whittled away the plants that cost too much or that you don't like, the remaining list should not be too mind-boggling.

BULBS FOR ADDED BEAUTY

Include a mix of tiny bulbs and spring flowers as well as a good number of summer-flowering plants. Little daffodils such as 'Minnow' and petticoat daffodil (*Narcissus bulbocodium*) are welcome in spring, along with dwarf crested iris (*Iris cristata*), windflowers (*Anemone blanda*), crocuses, and grape hyacinths (*Muscari* spp). Heaths and heathers are striking in rock gardens if the soil and climate will support them. And don't look just for flowers—interesting foliage can be just as eye-catching, and lasts longer.

RIGHT: Pink sedum and creeping Jenny spill like foam over a rocky edge. OPPOSITE: Broadleaf evergreens are overshadowed by small conifers glowing in green, gold, and blue. Each plant is clearly delineated against the gravel base, a look borrowed from Japanese rock gardens.

Look for a few plants or shrubs that will either flower in the autumn or display autumn color—compact grasses can often provide fall and winter interest, for example.

EVERGREEN ACCENTS

Be sure to plant a few dwarf and creeping conifers to accent your rock garden, and perhaps a few larger conifers with striking form to provide winter interest. Examples of these are lace-bark pine (*Pinus bungeana*), with branches trimmed up so the decorative bark is visible; the very narrow common juniper (*Juniperus communis* 'Pencil Point', sometimes called 'Sentinel'); the Korean fir (*Abies koreana* 'Silberlocke') with recurved, silvery needles; the unusual Japanese black pine (*Pinus thunbergiana* 'Thunderhead'); or the Japanese red pine (*Pinus densiflora* 'Umbraculifera'). Small boxwoods or other compact broadleaf evergreens also stretch out the season in a rock garden. Some other interesting plants to consider might be bearberry (*Arctostaphylos uva-ursi*) or wintergreen (*Gaultheria procumbens*), both of which are attractive all year. A few shrubs can be effective accents, especially varieties of cotoneaster or others with interesting forms. A rock garden can be the perfect place to frame a single weeping tree—structure and form are always key ingredients in a rock garden, and a few taller features will give the garden some focus when winter comes.

Water Gardens in Small Spaces

LITTLE PONDS AND WATER GARDENS IN CONTAINERS

Chapter 8

ABOVE: A small garden statue contributes to the peaceful aura of this lily pond. For a natural look, don't forget to choose plants for the area beside your water garden.

OPPOSITE: A water garden in a sink—what could be more natural? The tall, slender plants that predominate here include cattails, Siberian iris, Isolepsis cernua, *and* Lindera obtusiloba.

At one time water gardens were the reserve of the wealthy, created in the form of elaborate fountains or waterfalls, well-stocked lakes, or formal lily ponds studded with classical statuary. Today any gardener with a few feet of space and five to six hours of sunlight can create a water garden for a fairly reasonable price. Be careful not to equate "small" with "simple," though; gardeners who jump into projects and hope a little TLC will get them through might find some "RPM" more effective: research, planning, and maintenance. The "dig now, pay later" philosophy can prove expensive when it applies to water gardening.

ABOVE: Bold and basic, this simple water garden packs a lot of punch into a very small space. Get your feet wet in a water garden this size before excavating your backyard to install a pond. OPPOSITE: In early April this small pond is aglow with the golden flowers of **Caltha palustris** *and the softer sheen of* **Acer palmatum** *'Dissectum'. When constructing your water garden, consider building a "shelf" near the edge so that you can plant marginals. Surrounding the pond with bog plants gives it a natural look, allowing the water feature to meld seamlessly with the rest of the landscape.*

DESIGN CONSIDERATIONS

What is it about water in a garden that most appeals to you—the sound of moving water or the serenity of a pond that is still and clear as a mirror? Is it the darting shadows of fish in deep water, the flashes of goldfish skimming the surface of a pond? Does your ideal garden include the formal lines of a geometric, concrete pool lit with jewel-toned tropical water lilies, or do you envision a curving pond with edges obscured by lush vegetation—the Taj Mahal or Walden Pond?

Whether your water garden is a container on a deck, porch, or balcony or a pond in the middle of the backyard, it is bound to become a focal point of the landscape. A badly designed water garden won't just fade into the background—it will stick out like a store thumb. Natural versus formal, architectural versus softly curving lines, fish versus flowers, the relationship of sun to shade and of the pond to the house—all of these factors need to be considered. Do you want the pond to be visible from the house, or a surprise waiting at the end of a winding path? Features such as stepping stones and bridges are most effective when they lead to a focal point such as an arbor, bench, or gazebo, so consider where your "path" will lead and decide whether you truly have enough space to include these features.

Concealed lighting—either waterproof lights submerged under the water or spotlights shining down from a nearby tree—can be very effective for highlighting flowers and fish; it should be installed by a licensed electrician.

WHICH WATER FEATURE?

Even very small gardens can incorporate a water feature; its form should be a personal decision based on what you want most from a water garden. Start small with a lined container and a plant or two if you want to try out water gardening before investing in a pond. If it's sound and movement that you want, a trickling waterfall or small fountain can do the trick. One small waterfall I saw consisted of copper sluices transporting a small flow of water through different levels of barrels. Though heavy, the amount of space this arrangement consumes is very small. Other small fountains direct the flow of water through a bamboo funnel, where it spills into a barrel or onto a stone. Tiny indoor fountains are also available, trickling over polished gravel set in ceramic bowls planted with bonsai. Other fountains are incorporated into sculptures and attached to outside walls, moving water with a pump and taking up a minimum of space. Ponds with still water can be installed in the ground or in containers of different sizes, colors, and materials. A formal, geometric pond might work very well in a narrow, walled city garden while a curving pond accented by water-loving grasses and perennials could bring a small suburban lot to life. A cluster of containerized water gardens in staggered sizes, reflecting clouds and sky, easily becomes the focal point of a roof garden. Consult experts regarding weight load for aboveground water gardens; for in-ground ponds, be sure to comply with local ordinances regarding fences and gates to keep children safely away from the water.

MATERIALS

When choosing a material for your water garden, consider the architecture of your house as well as decks and gazebos, walls and fences; the type of water garden you select should blend with these features as well as with the landscape design. The shape of a pond and the type of materials used to edge it should blend with existing features as seamlessly as possible.

There is a vast array of materials from which to choose. Containerized water gardens come in styles ranging from lined wooden barrels and galvanized metal tubs to faux terra-cotta planters and black cauldrons. Ponds can be lined with preformed fiberglass, concrete, PVC (polyvinyl chloride), Butyl, or fish-grade EPDM (ethylene propylene diene monomer) synthetic rubber. Concrete, for a long time the standard material for lining ponds, is long-lasting but other materials are more flexible and less expensive. Whatever material is used, the pond will require periodic repairs and maintenance.

Popular edgings include wood decking, rough stone or stone slabs, concrete, tile, or plants. You'll want to match your edging to the character of your pond and the landscape that surrounds it—a naturalistic

Running water is a feature that will enhance any water garden. The gentle splashing sound of water trickling from a pump or flowing over stones soothes frayed nerves and distracts from distant sounds. This ingenious water garden includes a raised island bed near the wall, which allows terrestrial plants like ferns and ivies to flourish alongside traditional water plants and marginals.

The still water of a pond, the soothing sound of a bubbling fountain—these and other water elements in a garden convey a feeling of peace. But no matter how big the pond is or how elaborate the fountain, without a surrounding of lush green plants and delicate flowers the water features would be about as exciting as a puddle on a driveway. It is easy to purchase preformed ponds, relatively inexpensive fountains, and even water garden containers like wooden barrels, but planning a water garden is not quite so easy. Even if you plan to install a water garden yourself, it might be a good idea to consult with a land-

Blue iris, also called blue flag, is a stunning flower for wet or boggy areas.

Water lilies are as essential to the water garden as roses are to the cottage garden.

scape architect. Size, depth, pumping requirements, and compatibility with the existing architecture and landscape are all important considerations. If fish will be sharing the water with plants, both the site and the type of plants will have to fit in with the life-sustaining requirements of the fish.

There are basically two types of plants to consider for water gardens—flowering plants that grow in (or float on) the water or near the water's edge, and foliage plants that either grow in water or don't mind getting their feet wet. The flowering plants tend to need more sun than the foliage plants, although even the foliage plants need a few hours of sunlight. It is important to select plants appropriate

for the type of water feature (pool, pond, container), making sure that each plant has sufficient oxygen and room to grow.

FLOWERING WATER PLANTS

BLUE IRIS (*Iris versicolor*) This native, blue-flowering plant is hardy in most areas. It should be planted in water up to 6 inches (15cm) deep, in full sun to part shade.

HARDY WATER LILIES (*Nymphaea* spp.) *These lilies require still water 6–18 inches (15–45cm) deep over the roots; blossoms generally float on the surface of the water. Flowers bloom in the morning and close in the afternoon.*
  'Arc en Ciel'—A hardy lily with pale pink flowers and foliage variegated in flecks of ivory, rose, and purple. It is a medium-to-large spreader and requires full sun.
  'James Brydon'—This fragrant, red-flowering plant is recommended for ponds and containers. It spreads 6–12 feet (1.8–3.6m) and will survive in full sun or part shade.
  'Perry's Fire Opal'—A recent introduction, this hardy plant spreads 6–12 feet (1.8–3.6m); its striking fuchsia flowers will bloom best in full sun.

edging in a formal garden will most likely look unfinished, while the strict borders and polished look of glazed ceramic tile may seem out of place in a wild garden.

SITE SELECTION
Before digging a hole or filling a container with water, take some time to evaluate your

site. Think, too, about what you want from your water garden. Plants like lotuses and water lilies need at least 5 to 6 hours of sunlight in order to bloom satisfactorily. Fish, on the other hand, could poach under the hot summer sun. Placing a fishpond too close to a shade tree is generally a poor idea because the falling leaves will litter the surface, clog

the pond, and kill the fish; instead use smaller shrubs to create an effective screen. Siting the pond where it will receive some shade from the house is another option.

If you long for the sound of trickling water, position a fountain or waterfall near a window; to make the most of still waters, place the pond within sight of the house,

'Texas Dawn'—An award winner whose fragrant yellow flowers have a long season of bloom. This medium-to-large spreader can take full sun to part shade.

'Walter Pagels'—This small- to medium-size hardy plant has white, slightly fragrant flowers and is suitable for containers. It grows best with 5–6 hours of full sun.

LOTUS (*Nelumbo nucifera*)—'Tuliplotus'—The tulip-shaped white flowers of this hardy plant reach up to 2 feet (60cm) above the soil. It takes 1 full year to become established, requiring at least 17.5 quarts (19.2l) of heavy topsoil, with still water 2–4 inches (5–10cm) above the soil.

TROPICAL WATER LILIES (*Nymphaea* spp.) *These tender plants tend to be extremely fragrant and have flowers that stand above the surface of the water. They require 6–18 inches (15–45cm) of water over the roots.*

'Blue Beauty'—With speckled foliage and abundant, fragrant lavender-blue flowers, this medium-to-large spreader is a real winner.

'Colorata'—This is the lily for small containers—it needs only 6 inches (15cm) of water over the plant, and it spreads from just

1 to 6 feet (30 to 180cm). It has blue flowers and green foliage.

'Jennifer Rebecca'—Recommended for hot climates, this rose-red water lily has bronze foliage; it is a medium-to-large spreader. Blooms from sundown to midmorning.

'Panama Pacific'—This lily has rosy purple flowers and speckled leaves. It is a small-to-medium spreader that often produces plantlets on its leaves late in the season

FOLIAGE WATER PLANTS

ARROWHEAD (*Sagittaria latifolia*)—The white flowers are attractive, but it is the foliage that makes this plant stand out. It remains upright to 2 feet (60cm) tall in 6 inches (15cm) of water.

CREEPING JENNY (*Lysimachia nummularia*)— A groundcover for the edge of a pond, this plant stands 3 inches (7.5cm) high; it needs to be planted in soil with up to 2 inches (5cm) of water.

DWARF UMBRELLA PALM (*Cyperus alternifolius* 'Gracilis') This small plant stands 2 feet (60cm) tall in just 2 inches (5cm) of water. It is suit-

able for small pools, ponds, and containers.

GRACEFUL CATTAIL (*Typha laxmanni*) This hardy plant stays upright to 4 feet (1.2m) tall when planted in up to a foot (30cm) of water. The cattails bloom in summer.

VARIEGATED SWEET FLAG (*Acorus calamus* 'Variegatus') The green-and-cream blades of this plant reach 3 feet (90cm) tall; it should be planted in soil with up to 6 inches (15cm) of water.

There are dozens of water lotus cultivars available, including the popular 'Alba'.

deck, or seating area. Don't forget practical considerations: is the proposed site accessible to a water faucet or an electrical outlet to accommodate pumps or lighting? If you plan to put a containerized water garden on a balcony, roof garden, or raised deck, first consult an engineer to make sure the container won't be too heavy for the structure.

For ponds set in the ground, ensure that drainage is good enough to prevent rainwater from puddling over the edges.

A POND FOR FISH

Water gardens intended to house fish must take into consideration the fishes' needs. The rule of thumb for stocking a pond is to add

two snails and either one 8-inch (20cm) or two 4-inch (10cm) fish for each square yard (8,362 sq cm) of surface water. Oxygenating plants should be added at a rate of one plant per square foot (929 sq cm) of surface water. If the pond or container has just been filled for the first time, you will probably need to condition the water to make it safe for fish.

Fish and plants don't always work together in home landscapes: fish prefer moving water while plants such as water lilies perform best in still water; while water lilies need full sun, fish are much happier in cool shade. Deep water (36 inches [90cm] or more) can provide the cooler temperatures preferred by colorful koi but it is about a foot (30cm) deeper than recommended for most water lilies. Since koi will eat many water plants, the two may not be compatible in smaller ponds. Ordinary goldfish do not need the same depths as koi and are not as destructive to plants. A small fish called *Gambusia affinis* is particularily useful for small ponds and containers because it feeds on mosquito larvae floating on the water's surface.

To help protect fish from marauding cats or raccoons, try constructing underwater caverns made out of rocks for shelter. Fish need to be fed small portions frequently during warm weather; they do not require feeding over the winter, but the feeding schedule should be resumed in the spring. Since fish may not survive in shallow ponds that could freeze, they should be moved to an aquarium and stored in an unheated garage for the winter. An alternative would be to slope one end of the pond to 3 feet (90cm) or more to prevent it from freezing. One precaution: some small

Darting fishes delight pond owners but don't work well with all water plants. Decide which is your top priority—ornamental water plants or fishes—and then plan your garden accordingly.

ponds and fountains are kept from freezing in the winter by the use of electric
pumps. While antifreeze may help keep
the water flowing, it will kill both plants
and fish.

A POND FOR FLOWERS

Of the flowering plants, water lilies and
lotus are the varieties most often used in
water gardens—both require full sun.
Tropical water lilies generally bloom from
June to October and have scalloped leaves;
blossoms rise a few inches above the surface
and may be day- or night-flowering.
Although usually fragrant and available in
more colors than hardy lilies, they will not
survive cold weather.

Hardy water lilies will survive the
winter if the roots are protected from
freezing; the lilies should be selected in
small- to medium-growing cultivars. The
flowers, which float on the surface of the
water, open during the day and range from
shades of white and yellow to pink and red;
leaves are round and smooth. The cultivar
'Marliac White' is recommended for its
longevity and ease of cultivation; the
hybrid *Nymphaea* × *helvola* is a dwarf
variety suitable for containerized water

RIGHT: *A small backyard is transformed into
a watery wonderland with the addition of an
oval pool. The shade provided by a small tree
helps to create a restful atmosphere, but realize
that falling leaves mean some extra
maintenance.* **OPPOSITE:** *The water lotus,*
Nelumbo nucifera, *rises up above the water to
show off its distinctive blooms.*

gardens. When danger of a hard frost is past plant hardy water lilies by putting heavy soil (clay rather than sand) and the root into a container. The crown of the root should rest slightly above the soil when planted, and should not be covered with soil. Cover the roots and rhizome with a thin layer of soil topped with sand or gravel and then burlap to hold the soil in place. When preparing a new pond, set the plant box in the bottom of the pool first, then add water slowly. Remove the burlap once the pond is full.

Planting depths range from 6 to 24 inches (15 to 60cm), depending on the type of pond and ultimate size and type of plant. Create platforms of brick or flat rocks stacked to various heights on the bottom of your pond so that you can accommodate the various depths of your chosen water plants. Lotus, with flowers that rise 1 to 7 feet (30 to 210cm) above the water surface, are cold-hardy and vigorous; plant the rhizome in a container with 17–19 quarts (16–18l) of heavy topsoil instead of directly into the pond. Tropical water lilies are best planted in containers holding 16 quarts (15l) of heavy garden soil. Tropical water lilies and lotus rhizomes should be positioned in the soil 2 inches (5cm) below the soil surface (plant lotus horizontally; tropical lilies upright) in a container covered in gravel, with the crown above the soil line. Tropical lilies prefer a depth of 6 to 18 inches (15 to 45cm) under the water while lotus should initially be planted in 4–6 inches (10–15cm) of water, later increas-

ing the depth to about 8 inches (20cm). Fertilize monthly with commercial plant food, following the manufacturer's guidelines.

FOLIAGE WATER PLANTS

All plants need water to survive, but some like it more than others. Certain plants make it possible for life to be sustained in ponds and containers, either by floating on the surface and providing shade that controls algae, or by growing beneath the surface and releasing oxygen into the water during the process of photosynthesis. The latter are called oxygenating plants, and these include hornwort (*Ceratophyllum demersum*) and fanwort (*Cabomba*

caroliniana). Examples of floating plants are water lettuce (*Pistia stratiotes*) and water hyacinth (*Eichhornia crassipes*).

Still other plants thrive at the edge of ponds or in shallow water, and are called marginals: yellow flag (*Iris pseudacorus*), Japanese primrose (*Primula japonica*), marsh marigold (*Caltha palustris*), Joe-Pye weed (*Eupatorium purpureum*), cardinal flower (*Lobelia cardinalis*), and sweet flag (*Acorus calamus*) are all excellent marginals.

Whether your water garden is planted with flowers or with foliage, remember to keep surface water and plants in balance. Plants should cover no more than 60 to 75 percent of the surface of the pond.

MAINTENANCE

Small ponds and water gardens in containers will need to be cleaned periodically, a chore that is best done in the spring as soon as it is warm enough to move the overwintering fish out of the pond temporarily (50°F [10°C] or above).

Fertilize hardy water lilies and repot them into larger containers at this time. Remove fallen leaves and other debris, draining or pumping water from the pond or container, if possible, to clean sediment. It is normal for a newly planted water garden to have a consistency similar to pea soup—cloudy and green. As oxygenating plants grow and begin to work, the water color will remain green but should gradually clear.

With just a little work, you can add the wonderful dimension of water to even the smallest garden.

PLANT HARDINESS ZONES

ZONE 1
ZONE 2
ZONE 3
ZONE 4
ZONE 5
ZONE 6
ZONE 7
ZONE 8
ZONE 9
ZONE 10
ZONE 11

If you are living outside North America, use the following chart
to determine your plant hardiness zone.

Range of Average Annual Minimum Temperatures for Each Zone

	Fahrenheit (°F)	Celsius (°C)
Zone 1	Below −50°	Below −45.6°
Zone 2	−50° to −40°	−45.6° to −40°
Zone 3	−40° to −30°	−40° to −34.4°
Zone 4	−30° to −20°	−34.4° to −28.9°
Zone 5	−20° to −10°	−28.9° to −23.3°
Zone 6	−10° to 0°	−23.3° to −17.8°
Zone 7	0° to 10°	−17.8° to −12.2°
Zone 8	10° to 20°	−12.2° to −6.7°
Zone 9	20° to 30°	−6.7° to −1.1°
Zone 10	30° to 40°	−1.1° to 4.4°
Zone 11	Above 40°	Above 4.4°

Sources

PLANTS

Bear Creek Nursery
PO Box 411
Northport, WA 99157
Specializes in cold-hardy fruit trees, shrubs, and berries.

Busse Gardens
13579 10th St. NW
Cokato, MN 55321
(612) 286-2654
Fabulous hardy perennial plants, including wildflowers, hostas, and heucheras.

Comstock Seed
8520 W. 4th St.
Reno, NV 89523
(702) 746-3681
Seed supplier for drought-tolerant native grasses and other plants of the Great Basin.

Edible Landscaping
PO Box 77
Afton, VA 22920
(804) 361-9134
Edible for you and the birds and other wildlife—many fruiting trees and shrubs.

Finch Blueberry Nursery
PO Box 699
Bailey, NC 27807
(919) 235-4664
Excellent selection of blueberries.

Forestfarm
990 Tetherow Road
Williams, OR 97544
(503) 846-7269
Catalog of more than two thousand plants, including Western natives, perennials, and an outstanding variety of trees and shrubs.

The Fragrant Path
PO Box 328
Ft. Calhoun, NE 68023
Seeds for fragrant annuals, perennials, shrubs, and vines, many of them old-fashioned favorites.

Gardens of the Blue Ridge
9056 Pittman Gap Road
PO Box 10
Pineola, NC 28662
Excellent selection of native trees and shrubs

Goodwin Creek Gardens
PO Box 83
Williams, OR 97544
(541) 846-7375
Specializes in herbs, everlasting flowers, and fragrant plants, as well as plants that attract butterflies and hummingbirds.

Holbrook Farm & Nursery
115 Lance Road
PO Box 368
Fletcher, NC 28732
Good selection of flowering shrubs.

Jackson & Perkins
PO Box 1028
Medford, OR 97501
(800) 292-4769
Fine selection of roses, perennials, and other garden-worthy plants.

Kurt Bluemel, Inc.
2740 Green Lane
Baldwin, MD 31013
Excellent selection of ornamental grasses, rushes, and sedges.

Lilypons Water Gardens
PO Box 10
6800 Lilypons Road
Buckeystown, MD 21717
(301) 874-5133
Plants and supplies for water gardens.

Morden Nurseries, Ltd.
PO Box 1270
Morden, MB
Canada R0G 1J0
Wide selection of ornamental trees and shrubs.

Niche Gardens
1111 Dawson Rd.
Chapel Hill, NC 27516
(919) 967-0078
Good, healthy plants of grasses, nursery-propagated wildflowers, perennials, and herbs.

Northwoods Nursery
27368 South Oglesby
Canby, OR 97013
503-266-5432
Ornamental trees, shrubs, and vines.

Prairie Moon Nursery
Rt. 3 Box 163
Winona, MN 55987
(507) 452-1362
Generously sized plants and seeds of native prairie grasses and wildflowers.

Prairie Nursery
PO Box 306
Westfield, WI 53964
(608) 296-3679
Catalog of prairie grasses and native wildflowers.

Santa Barbara Heirloom Seedling Nursery
PO Box 4235
Santa Barbara, CA 93140
(805) 968-5444
Organically grown heirloom seedlings of vegetables, herbs, and edible flowers.

Shady Oaks Nursery
112 10th Ave. SE
Waseca, MN 56093
(507) 835-5033
Specializes in plants that thrive in shade, including wildflowers, ferns, perennials, shrubs, and others.

Shepherd's Garden Seeds
30 Irene Street
Torrington, CT 06790
(860) 482-0532
Fine selection of annuals, perennials, vegetables, and herbs.

Southwestern Native Seeds
PO Box 50503
Tucson, AZ 85703
Responsibly collected wildflower seeds from the Southwest, West, and Mexico.

Sunlight Gardens
Rt. 1 Box 600-A
Hillvale Rd.
Andersonville, TN 37705
(615) 494-8237
Wonderful selection of wildflowers, all nursery propagated.

Tripple Brook Farm
37 Middle Rd.
Southampton, MA 01073
(413) 527-4626
Wildflowers and other Northeastern native plants, along with fruits and shrubs.

Van Engelen Inc.
23 Tulip Drive
Bantam, CT 06750
Wide variety of bulbs.

Van Ness Water Gardens
2460 N. Euclid Ave.
Upland, CA 91786
(909) 982-2425
Everything you could possibly need for a water garden, from plants to pools to supplies.

Vermont Wildflower Farm
Rt. 7
Charlotte, VT 05445
(802) 425-3500
Excellent wildflower seed and seed mixes.

Wayside Gardens
Garden Lande
Hodges, SC 29695
Offers a wide array of bulbs and perennials.

We-Du Nurseries
Rt. 5 Box 724
Marion, NC 28752
(704) 738-8300
Incredible variety of wildflowers and native perennials from several continents, many woodland plants.

Westgate Garden Nursery
751 Westgate Drive
Eureka, CA 95503
Large selection of rhododendrons and unusual ornamental shrubs and trees.

White Flower Farm
PO Box 50
Litchfield, CT 06759
(800) 503-9624
Good selection of plants, including hostas, ferns, and hellebores.

Wildlife Nurseries
PO Box 2724
Oshkosh, WI 54903
(414) 231-3780
Plants and seeds of native grasses, annuals, and perennials for wildlife. Also water garden plants and supplies.

Wildwood Gardens
14488 Rock Creek Road
Chardon, OH 44024
Collector's list of dwarf conifers and other dwarf shrubs.

Woodlanders, Inc.
1128 Colleton Ave.
Aiken, SC 29801
(803) 648-7522
Excellent selection of native trees, shrubs, ferns, vines, and perennials, plus other good garden plants.

Yucca Do Nursery
PO Box 655
Waller, TX 77484
(409) 826-6363
Good selection of trees, shrubs, and perennial plants, including many natives.

GARDEN FEATURES

Anderson Design
PO Box 4057 C
Bellingham, WA 98227
(800) 947-7697
Arbors, trellises, gates, and pyramids (Oriental, modern, and traditional style).

Bamboo Fencer
31 Germania Street
Jamaica Plain, Boston, MA 02130
(617) 524-6137
Bamboo fences.

Barlow Tyrie Inc.
1263 Glen Avenue Suite 230
Moorestown, NJ 08057-1139
(609) 273-7878
Teak wood garden furniture in English garden style.

Boston Turning Works
42 Plymouth Street
Boston, MA 02118
(617) 482-9085
Distinctive wood finials for gates, fenceposts, and balustrades.

Brooks Barrel Company
PO Box 1056
Department GD25
Cambridge, MD 21613-1046
(410) 228-0790
Natural-finish pine wooden barrels and planters.

Charleston Gardens
61 Queen Street
Charleston, SC 29401
(803) 723-0252
Fine garden furnishings.

Doner Design Inc.
DepartmentG
2175 Beaver Valley Pike
New Providence, PA 17560
(717) 786-8891
Handcrafted copper landscape lights.

Florentine Craftsmen Inc.
46-24 28th Street
DepartmentGD
Long Island City, NY 11101
(718) 937-7632
Garden furniture, ornaments, fountains and statuary of lead, stone, and bronze.

Flower Framers by Jay
671 Wilmer Avenue
Cincinnati, Ohio 45226
Flower boxes.

FrenchWyres
PO Box 131655
Tyler, TX 75713
(903) 597-8322
Wire garden furnishings: trellis, urns, cachepots, window boxes, arches, and plant stands.

Gardenia
9 Remington Street
Cambridge, MA 02138
(800) 685-8866
Birdhouses.

Gardensheds
651 Millcross Road
Lancaster, PA 17601
Potting sheds, wood boxes, and larger storage units.

Hooks Lattice
7949 Silverton Avenue #903
San Diego, CA 92126
(800) 896-0978
Handcrafted wrought-iron gardenware.

Kenneth Lynch & Sons
84 Danbury ROad
PO Box 488
Wilton, CT 06897
(203) 762-8363
Benches, gates, scupture and statuary, planters and urns, topiary, sundials, and weathervanes.

Kinsman Company
River Road
Department351
Point Pleasant, PA 18950
(800) 733-4146
European plant supports, pillars, arches trellises, flowerpots, and planters.

Lake Creek Garden Features Inc.
PO Box 118
Lake City, IA 51449
(712) 464-8924
Obelisks, plant stands, and gazing globes and stands.

Liteform Designs
PO Box 3316
Portland, OR 97208
(503) 253-1210
Garden lighting: path, bullard, accent, step, and tree fixtures.

New Blue Moon Studio
PO Box 579
Leavenworth, WA 98826
(509) 548-4754
Trellises, gates, arbors, and garden furniture.

New England Garden Ornaments
PO Box 235
38 East Brookfield Road
North Brookfield, MA 01535
(508) 867-4474
Garden fountains and statuary, planters and urns, antique furniture, sundials, and limestone ornaments.

Secret Garden
c/o Christine Sibley
15 Waddell Street N.E.
Atlanta, GA 30307
Garden sculpture.

Stone Forest
Department G
P.O. Box 2840
Sante Fe, NM 87504
(505) 986-8883
Hand-carved granite birdbaths, basins, fountains, lanterns, and spheres.

Sycamore Creek
PO Box 16
Ancram, NY 12502
Handcrafted copper garden furnishings.

Tanglewood Conservatories
Silver Spring, MD
Handcrafted period glass houses and atriums.

Tidewater Workshop
Oceanville, NJ 08231
(800) 666-8433
White cedar benches, chairs, swings, and tables.

Toscano
17 East Campbell Street
Department G881
Arlington Heights, IL 60005
(800) 525-1733
Historic garden sculptures, including seraphs and cherubs.

Valcovic Cornell Design
Box 380
Beverly, MA 01915
Trellises and arbor benches (traditional to contemporary styles).

Vixen Hill Manufacturing Company
Main Street
Elverson, PA 19520
(800) 423-2766
Cedar gazebos and screened garden houses.

Weatherend Estate Furniture
6 Gordon Drive
Rockland, ME 04841
(800) 456-6483
Heirloom-quality garden furniture.

Wood Classics
Box 96G0410
Gardiner, NY 12525
(914) 255-5651
Garden benches, swings, chairs and tables, rockers, lounges, and umbrellas (all teak and mahogany outdoor furniture).

AUSTRALIA

Country Farm Perennials
RSD Laings Road
Nayook VIC 3821

Cox's Nursery
RMB 216 Oaks Road
Thrilmere NSW 2572

Honeysuckle Cottage Nursery
Lot 35 Bowen Mountain Road
Bowen Mountain via Grosevale NSW 2753

Swan Bros Pty Ltd
490 Galston Road
Dural NSW 2158

CANADA

Corn Hill Nursery Ltd.
RR 5
Petitcodiac NB EOA 2HO

Ferncliff Gardens
SS 1
Mission, British Columbia
V2V 5V6

McFayden Seed Co. Ltd.
Box 1800
Brandon, Manitoba
R7A 6N4

Stirling Perennials
RR 1
Morpeth, Ontario
N0P 1X0

Index

Photography Credits